EXOTIC FEASTS

By the same author:

Indonesian Food and Cookery (Prospect Books)
Indonesian and Thai Cookery (Piatkus)
The Cooking of Thailand, Indonesia and Malaysia
(Martin Books for Sainsburys)

EXOTIC
FEASTS

Sri Owen's
Book of
Seasonal Menus

KYLE CATHIE

To the memory of my paternal grandmother
and my parents

First published 1991 by
Kyle Cathie Limited
3 Vincent Square London SW1P 2LX

ISBN 1 85626 036 4

Illustrated by Soun Vannithone

A Cataloguing in Publication record for this title is available from the
British Library

Designed by Beverley Waldron
Typeset by Rowland Phototypesetting Ltd
Bury St Edmunds, Suffolk
Printed and bound in Great Britain by
Butler & Tanner Ltd, Frome, Somerset

Contents

Acknowledgments

I want to thank a great many good friends, old and new, for their advice, help, encouragement and willingness to act as guinea pigs when I was testing recipes. I particularly want to name those who have allowed me to use recipes from their books or private collections, in many cases for dishes they themselves have developed and perfected, and those whose advice I have so often sought. They are, in random order, Yan-kit So, Geraldene Holt, Jenny Coaker, Shaun Hill, Ann and Franco Taruschio, Anne Willan, Heidi Lascelles, Maggie Black, David Wilkinson, Kate Riley, Silvija Davidson, the Blue Elephant restaurant, Vicky Jones, of *House and Garden*, in which several of these recipes first appeared, Lan Anh Phung, Linda Sue Park, Alice Wooledge Salmon, and Alan Davidson, for permission to use material from Phia Sing's *Traditional Recipes of Laos*.

I have been greatly helped by the understanding and professional expertise of my agent, Caroline Davidson, my publisher, Kyle Cathie, and my editor, Annie Jackson. My particular thanks go to my husband, Roger, for his all-round assistance and support.

Introduction

I LOVE GOOD food and I love cooking. I also love travelling. The differences between countries and people are a continual source of surprise and pleasure. My favourite dishes are those that match contrasting tastes and textures so that they keep their separate characters but combine agreeably together, like the oil, vinegar and garlic that dress a crisp green salad.

I was in my late twenties when I came to Europe from Indonesia for the first time, but I had read a lot of English novels and tried my hand at cooking a few classic French and Italian dishes: chicken Marengo, saltimbocca, recipes whose ingredients could be supplied from the local marketplace. As soon as I was settled in my new home, I started to explore cookbooks and food shops. I have never stopped exploring, but since I started to write about food my researches have become more clearly focused and perhaps a little better organised. A new book is not a final arrival, but another stage on the journey. Writing this one has helped me to clarify my ideas, forced me to be precise in my cooking and testing, suggested new lines of enquiry. Because it was an adventure for me, I hope you, too, will find it adventurous.

The purpose of this book is to show how dishes from opposite sides of the world can combine happily together on the same table. In flavours, recipes and techniques, the traditions of East and West enhance each other. I have included, as part of this Introduction, notes about the ingredients you will need; some of them may be unfamiliar to you, but all are now generally available in most European, Australian and North American cities – in fact I am no longer surprised when I find quite exotic products in little corner shops and village stores. Likewise, ingredients for the western recipes can all be found in Asian supermarkets and shopping centres without difficulty.

3

I hope this book will appeal to people in both East and West, and that Asian readers will find it useful, even though their attitude to western food is likely to be different from westerners' attitudes to the exotic spices of the Orient. I must say straight away, however, that I have written this book from a mainly western viewpoint, and for that reason I have put more emphasis on western styles of cooking. I don't claim that my recipes are in every case 'authentic' (whatever that word means). I ceased to be a traditionalist a long time ago. But readers – East or West – who cook their way through these menus will become familiar with the tastes and techniques of several cuisines, and will be well-placed to explore more widely and deeply.

Although these menus evolved during many years of my life in London, the book has also grown out of the visits I've made from time to time to my old home and to other countries of South-East Asia.

There, the ways people cook and eat are changing radically. Like fashions in clothes, food fashions change, though the forces that drive them are more complex. As people move out of the countryside and into white-collar jobs in the cities, their eating habits are likely to be quite different from those of their parents. They have more money, but less time. Their families are smaller and they may quickly lose touch with cousins and more distant relatives, but they know more about the world outside and they don't want to feel left behind by it. And yet they are just as conservative as people anywhere else, so the old dishes remain as popular as ever, even if they are not made in quite the same way. These new families, in which husband and wife both have full-time jobs, want to be able to cook a meal quickly and serve it European-style. So a lot of traditional recipes that I brought with me from Indonesia in the sixties have changed and developed even in Indonesia itself, and the same process is going on in other countries.

I dare say this could have been said about middle-class city folk at any time since 1900 or so, but until recently they were a very small group in most Asian countries. Nowadays they are numerous and they have money to spend. As a result, you can now find in Jakarta, Manila or Taipei all the things we associate with such a class: smart restaurants (often in five-star hotels), well-equipped kitchens with electric ovens in flats and houses, gourmet magazines, cookery programmes on TV, supermarkets and delicatessens, and imported goodies at high prices. You may think these developments are good, or bad, or a mixture, but they all go together.

Another change surprised me more: in many Asian countries today rice consumption, per head, is falling – in some areas it is barely half what it was twenty years ago. For various reasons, governments have encouraged their populations to eat more bread or potatoes. Until quite recently, potatoes were used like any other vegetable, as something to fill the pot, not as the basis for a meal. Today they have become more versatile. At the same time, the spread of American fast-food chains has encouraged young people to regard french fries as the smart thing to order. Asian parents have always been rather indulgent towards their children in matters of food, and nowadays, if the whole family eats out, it is often the children who decide what sort of place they should go to.

Noodles, on the other hand, have been standard fare all over this region for a very long time. The Chinese, who grow large amounts of wheat in areas where rice cannot flourish, have been making noodles for at least as long as the Italians have made pasta. They have many of the virtues of rice – they are easy to cook, nourishing, they take up the flavour of whatever you eat them with, and they absorb a certain amount of the sauces on the plate. Some of my first contacts with Italian food were through pasta and risotto; I now find that rice, noodles, pasta or potatoes all make equally good accompaniments to the dishes described here.

From the western reader's point of view, then, what is South-East Asian food all about? Amid all this flurry of change, what are the more or less fixed landmarks, and which of these are likely to be sympathetically received in the West?

To start with, of course, South-East Asian food is often strongly-flavoured. I first wrote 'spicy', but spices have too many different flavours for that single adjective to mean much, and anyway the strong flavours come from other substances too, often fermented, sometimes very salty. The major source of protein in the average peasant's diet has always been salted fish, and in most countries of the region you will find some sort of concentrated essence of salt fish being used as a basic ingredient in sauces and meat dishes. In the notes that follow this Introduction, you will find it under the names 'Fish sauce' and 'Shrimp paste'. These are not interchangeable, by the way – you can't use one as a substitute for the other. Soy sauce is another fairly common factor in the cooking of this diverse region; it, too, is extremely salty, though its flavour is unlike anything made from fish.

The other strong flavour that westerners associate, often rather nervously, with South-East Asian food is chilli peppers. Many Englishmen, and virtually all Texans, seem to regard tolerance for the hottest chillies as a symbol of their virility. Where I grew up, we all took chillies for granted and were pretty well addicted to them from about the age of eleven. I am no exception to this, I love chillies, the hotter the better, but I do not pretend that European food is bland without them or that Asian food has to be heavily dosed with them. On the other hand, quite apart from hotness, chillies have a characteristic flavour that is found in no other spice. The recipes in this book contain just enough chilli to give flavour without causing even mild discomfort. If you like your food really hot, add more, or serve a hot chilli sauce.

The contrast between chilli-hot and salty is one dimension of South-East Asian food. Another is the contrast between sour and sweet. Sweetness comes from the natural sugars found, above all, in the coconut, though palm sugar, banana flowers and bamboo shoots are other sources. Sourness comes from vinegar, certain sour-tasting fruits (for example, tamarind), or from a range of citrus fruit and citrusy-tasting plants, of which the most important and useful is lemon grass. The familiar, over-sweetened 'sweet-and-sour' sauces that we know all too well from anglicised Chinese restaurants do not feature in good cooking anywhere, and certainly not in this book.

Something else that doesn't appear in this book but is used almost universally by cooks east of Calcutta (or thereabouts) is monosodium glutamate. This is a synthetic flavouring which reproduces a chemical compound found naturally in a type of Japanese seaweed; the chemical was isolated by a Japanese chemist in 1904 and is now manufactured in vast, almost incomprehensible quantities. The Japanese call it *aji-no-moto*. It has almost no flavour of its own, but acts on the tastebuds to make them more sensitive to whatever savoury substance is in the mouth at the time. It therefore makes indifferent food taste better than it really is. Most people will tell you that a little pinch does no harm, and most western food manufacturers and processors list it among the raw materials of their products. However, many people, including myself, are highly allergic to it. Cooks, especially in Asian restaurants where materials may be of poor quality, spoon it in lavishly. When I was a guest chef at a famous London hotel a few years ago, I had two charming and extremely able Thai sous-chefs to help me; they were excellent cooks, but I had the greatest difficulty in persuading them that their 'magic powder' was unnecessary and could be harmful to some of their customers. If your materials are good, your quantities right and your method sound, MSG can add nothing to your cooking but it can make you or your guests ill.

And what of spices, whose pungent scents and bizarre flavours were a basis of trade among eastern peoples centuries before any European ever sailed to the Indies? The spices of the Moluccas were, in a sense, our undoing; they attracted European traders who fought among themselves and too soon became colonisers instead of merchants. But that time is over, and the spices still have their mysterious powers. They not only taste delicious, each in its own very individual way, but they blend together as variously and beautifully as the instruments of an orchestra; they preserve food; they excite appetite and they aid digestion. One of the benefits of modern transport should be that you can buy fresh spices anywhere in the world. In practice it is often difficult to know how fresh the contents of the supermarket spice rack really are; their shelf-life is not as long as optimistic shopkeepers think. Old spices will not do you any harm, but they lose flavour as they age. When possible, buy unground, uncut, unmixed spices and grind and blend them yourself.

Finally, there is the foundation, glory and ornament of Asian food: rice. Throughout most of South-East Asia this means long-grain rice, the classic breed (among the countless thousands of varieties that exist) being Thai fragrant or jasmine rice; unlike Patna and Basmati, it is slightly sticky and therefore convenient to eat with the fingers, which is what I was brought up to do. It also remains slightly absorbent when cooked, so that it takes up whatever sauces it finds on the plate, softening and blending flavours against its own unassertive background and providing the basic texture of the meal. Western shops now offer an increasing choice of rices, each particularly suited to a different purpose or treatment, and the steady expansion of choice in the ingredients of good food is one of the more hopeful signs of our times.

This book is arranged as a series of menus to fit, more or less, the seasons of Europe and North America. Elsewhere, in countries with different climates, the seasonal headings can of course be ignored; what matters is that you should be able to get the ingredients.

Any of the main dishes in the menus, as well as any of the main-course dishes described in the last section of the book, can be served with rice, noodles or potatoes as a complete 'one-dish' meal.

The full menus have been organised and tested carefully to provide really interesting and satisfying meals which are quick and convenient to prepare. Naturally, any of these menus can be varied, and dishes from other menus or from the final part of the book can be substituted or added. But I would suggest that when you first prepare any of the menus you avoid making unnecessary changes. The second time round, you will know how things fit together and what changes you can make, if you want to.

People often ask me what they should drink with this kind of food. 'Champagne, definitely – right through the meal' is, I find, a popular answer, and is actually quite good advice. But in fact any decent wine, red or white, will go perfectly well with the dishes described here, and you should be guided by your own taste. There is nothing in this book so strongly-flavoured that it will kill anything that is drunk with it, though you do need a good fruity white with a salmon and mango salad, and most of the desserts will go better with a dessert wine than with whatever happens to be left over from earlier in the evening. I myself was brought up to drink nothing with a meal – not even water – but that isn't a rule I would want to impose on anyone else. In South-East Asia itself, one tends to drink beer rather than wine because good beers are brewed locally.

One last point – I emphasise simplicity and convenience in all these menus, and if you are cooking for two or four people this usually means that preparation and cooking times are short. When it comes to cooking for a party of twelve or sixteen, however, everything is bound to take longer. So, if you have invited a lot of people round, do work out your kitchen schedule in advance and budget your time. You will still find that a lot of the preparation can be done a day or more ahead. Then, on the night, make sure that you enjoy the food and conversation as much as your guests do.

Ingredients

Precise instructions for using these ingredients are contained in the recipes; these notes give some general information, and suggest where they can be bought.

Bamboo shoots

Canned bamboo shoots are sold in almost all ethnic foodstores and some supermarkets. They are either in chunks, or already sliced; there is even one brand now which stamps sliced bamboo shoots into fancy shapes. You can often find young shoots in glass jars as well as in cans. If you don't use the contents of a can at one go, you can keep the leftovers in the fridge, in a jar – not in the can – for up to a week, provided the shoots are covered in water.

Bananas

The banana is a far more interesting and varied fruit than you would ever guess from the European supermarket variety. One or two of the big chains, it's true, are experimenting with the miniature fig sucrier bananas, which are very sweet, red cooking bananas, and the big green plantains – these too are cooked and eaten as vegetables. Most of the very best varieties are unsuitable for mass shipment and warehouse ripening. The Gros Michel bananas which we usually get in Europe are, though not ideal, quite suitable for frying in batter and for other dessert or tea-time dishes.

Among the commonest, yet most ornamental, sights in any village or suburb in the tropics are the banana trees; every house seems to have two or three in its back yard, and because the trees grow, fruit and are cut back to ground level all within twelve months they provide a constantly changing prospect. Their wide, flat leaves can be cut when young and used as plates, food wrappers, or containers for cooking (you can buy fresh or frozen banana leaves in many ethnic food shops in England, though there is no dish in this book that really needs them). As the tree matures, wind shreds the leaves into strips that flutter cheerfully. The main stem produces a single large flower, whose outer petals lift, one by one, to reveal the embryonic combs of bananas under them. Only the first few are allowed to develop; then the flower is cut off, so that the bananas will be large and sweet. The cut flower is cooked and eaten as a vegetable; canned banana flowers are exported.

Basil

The Thais use two kinds of basil; one is green-stemmed, the stems of the other are dark purple. The first of these is what people in the West call 'sweet' basil, or very like it; it is used in, for instance, pesto sauce in Italy. It is perfectly all right for some oriental dishes, e.g. chilli beef with fried basil (page 180), but the purple-stemmed kind is usually much better if you can get it. In London, the Thai food shops get a weekly batch of it by air from Bangkok in time for the week-end. This basil has a lovely minty smell and flavour.

Beancurd – see Tofu

Beancurd skins

These are sold in many Thai, Chinese and Japanese food shops. The skin, made from soya beans, is soft and pliable and can be easily cut with scissors. In this book, it is used in Golden Parcels (page 157).

Beans – see Yard-long beans

Beansprouts

These can often be found in small greengrocers as well as supermarkets, and of course ethnic shops. They will keep for a day or two in the fridge. For certain dishes, it is worth spending time to break off the little brown root on each sprout – it doesn't affect the taste but it enhances the appearance of, for example, a salad.

Candlenuts

Candlenuts are sometimes obtainable in good Asian food shops; some Thai and Chinese shops sell vacuum-packed nuts. They are mildly toxic if eaten raw, but perfectly safe when cooked. Macadamia nuts are smaller but similar in appearance and taste, and easier to find. If even these are not available, almonds will do in most cases.

Cardamom

Some people prefer the spelling 'cardamon' or 'cardamun'. There are several varieties, indeed two different species of plant provide these strong-smelling seeds. By the time they get to market, the only noticeable distinction is that some are light-greenish, others almost black. It doesn't really make any difference which you use. They are normally put into the pot whole, so try to fish them out before they end up on guests' plates.

Chillies

Chillies come in many sizes and strengths and mostly in two colours, green and red. They are quite easy to find nowadays, though if you want the small 'bird chillies' you will probably have to go to an Asian shop because they are too hot for most westerners. The smaller the chilli, the hotter it is; the big ones, red and green, are pretty mild. The hottest part of the chilli is the seeds, which are therefore often removed before cooking. Chillies can irritate your skin if you are not used to handling them, but you can protect yourself by rubbing a little salt on your hands before you start and, of course, washing them well when you have finished. Keep your hands away from your face and eyes. If you get a tiny drop of chilli juice in your eye, wash the eye in plenty of cold water; it will be uncomfortable only for a short time.

Chinese cabbage

Chinese cabbage, Chinese leaves: these are the same thing. They are pretty generally obtainable in supermarkets and Asian shops.

Chinese chives

These resemble 'ordinary' chives but are larger and stronger-tasting. Most Asian shops should stock them.

Coconut

South-East Asia would be unimaginable without coconuts, but we regard them as a vital ingredient of savoury dishes just as much as of sweets. Directions for using coconuts and making coconut milk will be found on page 27.

Coriander leaves

These are now becoming so easy to find – in ethnic shops, greengrocers and supermarkets – that they are almost a standard herb, like parsley.

Cream

This is not as alien to Asian cooking as you may think, now that countries like Thailand and Indonesia are raising herds of dairy cows and acquiring a taste for butter and cheese. There is a widely-held belief that most, if not all, Asians lack the enzymes in their stomachs necessary to digest milk; but I think that most of them have simply not been used to milk and don't like it much when they first try it. In India, of course, butter (in the form of *ghee*) and yogurt are used a lot in cooking. I have found cream and yogurt excellent substitutes for coconut milk, not merely taking its place but adding texture and flavour that coconut milk doesn't provide; however, I have no time for cooks who ladle cream into every sauce, presumably in the belief that if a little is sometimes good a lot must always be better.

Fish sauce

Most South-East Asian cuisines have some kind of strongly-flavoured, ultra-salty fish-based seasoning. In Indonesia and Malaysia it is a solid, pungent block (see *Shrimp paste*). In Thailand, Laos and Vietnam it is liquid, obtainable in bottles in all Asian shops; the Thais call it *nam pla* (and I have used this name in some recipes), the Vietnamese call it *nuoc mam*, the Laotians *nam pa*. It keeps indefinitely. Use it sparingly.

Five-spice powder

The five spices vary, but normally include: cassia bark, cloves, fennel and star anise; the fifth may be ginger or Szechuan pepper. In any case, the result has a strong liquorice-like flavour. Use sparingly.

Galingale (galangal or laos)

This is the picturesque old English name for a root, looking rather like ginger but much more pink-and-white in colour, which gives dishes its own characteristic bitter flavour. It is fairly easily obtainable in Thai (*ka*) and Chinese shops. Like many spices, it has a limited shelf-life in its natural form, and it is therefore dried and ground into powder, which retains much (though really not all) of the flavour of the fresh root. The powder is also of course more convenient to store and to use. Furthermore, the powder vanishes into the sauce during cooking, whereas the root must be taken out and discarded before the dish is served; to bite into a chunk of galingale that has been overlooked can be a slightly unnerving experience, especially if you have no idea what it is.

Ginger

Many of these recipes specify fresh ginger – i.e. the root, which should be peeled, then either chopped or sliced finely. The finely-chopped ginger can be measured in a teaspoon. Some recipes will specify that the ginger is to be put in the blender to be blended with other spices to make a paste. Ginger is widely available in most high-street greengrocers and supermarkets as well as ethnic shops.

Glucose

Glucose is sold as a thick, colourless syrup. It is less sweet than white sugar, and rather similar to golden syrup, which has a high glucose content. It is used in the recipe for Black Glutinous Rice Sorbet (page 140) to give the sorbet a smoother texture. You can buy this from a chemist.

Groundnuts – see Nuts

Kaffir lime leaf

These are obtainable, fresh or dried, from most Thai and other oriental food shops. They are used frequently in South-East Asian cooking because they give the food a nice citrus tang.

Lemon grass

This herb, which does look like a coarse, heavy type of grass, is used in many recipes for its mildly sour-sweet, citrusy flavour. It can be bought, fresh, dried or ground, in many Asian shops and some supermarkets. It may sometimes be persuaded to grow as a house plant. Put a stem in water; if, with luck, it starts to grow roots, pot it in compost in a good-sized pot (once it is established, don't try to 'pot it on' or move it). Keep it on a windowsill in a warm sunny spot, or in a greenhouse; in warm summer weather it can safely be moved out of doors. Don't try to harvest it until it is well settled in and growing vigorously – this will take two to three months at least. To get a fresh stem of lemon grass for your cooking, carefully pull off just one stem; the plant will regenerate what it has lost quite easily, provided you don't push it too hard. Lemon grass is sold in stems about 15 cm (6 inch) long, with the tough but fragrant outer leaves trimmed short. For most dishes cut the stem into three equal lengths; one of these pieces is usually sufficient. Remember to remove it before serving. For curries, the outer leaves are stripped off and discarded and only the tender heart is used, chopped into little rounds like a spring onion and added to other spices to be blended into a curry paste. Prepare in the same way for salad dressing and use these tiny thin slices raw.

Lemons and limes

Although these are (obviously) two different fruits, they are so nearly related, and so alike in their sharp citrusy flavour, that they are pretty well interchangeable, and in most of my recipes I have simply given them as alternatives.

Macadamia nuts

These are a good substitute for candlenuts. They are sold fairly widely, usually roasted and salted – which is a pity, because they are nicer when freshly shelled, but they are still OK for cooking. Some supermarkets sell them in their shells, at any rate before Christmas. The shells are very, very hard indeed, and even with ratchet nutcrackers you need a powerful grip.

Mirin

A kind of Japanese rice cooking wine; you can buy it in most Chinese and Japanese shops. Dry sherry or dry white wine or Shaohsing wine will take its place quite satisfactorily.

Nam pla – see Fish sauce

Noodles

As with pasta, there are many types. Noodles and pasta are in fact almost the same thing, and if you prefer pasta, or have difficulty getting noodles, then you can regard them as interchangeable. To my palate, and much as I love Italian food, noodles are less stodgy. Cooking times and methods are the same for both – basically, three minutes in boiling water. The three types of noodle mentioned in this book are:

Egg noodles
These are egg-yellow and are sold in brick-shaped packets containing smaller blocks, each a tangled mass of noodles. In section, they may be round or flat. You can sometimes buy fresh ones in Chinese shops, but the dried packeted ones are really just as good. They keep for months.

Rice vermicelli
These are made from rice flour. The thick, flattish ribbons are also called rice sticks; thin ones, like bundles of wire, are the ones normally used in soup.

Cellophane noodles
These, like the second type of rice vermicelli, resemble bundles of thin, translucent wires. They are made from mung beans.

Nuts

Nuts play, I think, a much larger role in everyone's diet in Asia than they do in the West. For one thing, they are plentiful and cheap; I remember eating cashews in Java as casually as I might eat peanuts in England. Tropical countries have a far greater variety of nuts than Europe, although, I must admit, no hazels, no walnuts; so Europeans may well feel they score on those. Some tropical nuts are much used in cooking, e.g. candlenuts and macadamia nuts, to which, in this list, I have granted special sections of their own. Peanuts and groundnuts are two names for the same thing. They are more like vegetables than tree-fruit, growing not on trees or large bushes but on small plants. These flower in the ordinary way, but the seed-pods then develop on long stalks which dive underground to mature. These nuts are always cultivated; there are no wild varieties, at any rate not in the Old World. Like chillies, and several other foods that one nowadays associates inseparably with tropical Asia, they came originally from central and south America, brought by Spanish and Portuguese explorers.

Oils

The standard oil for cooking in tropical South-East Asia is of course coconut oil, but groundnut oil and corn oil are also commonly used. We don't grow olives, but we import a certain amount of olive oil, and I use it often in England. For the dishes in this book, I would say that it doesn't make a lot of difference which oil you use; just take the one you have on the shelf. My preference is for olive oil.

Okra

You can now find okra or ladies' fingers in many supermarkets. Yet they are still considered an acquired taste, perhaps because they have a rather slimy texture. They should therefore be served hot, straight from the pan, and eaten straight away. They are more commonly used in Indian cooking, but people in South-East Asia eat them as well. Choose young ones, not much more than 10 cm (4 inches) long, and to prepare them simply trim off a little at the stem end, which is rather hard.

Pak choy

This Chinese vegetable, small, with white, bunched-together stalks and broad, fleshy spoon-shaped leaves, is slowly becoming easier to find but is still rare outside ethnic shops.

Palm sugar

This is a dark reddish-brown substance, made from the juice of the coconut-palm flower. Almost all Asian food stores sell it; it is sometimes called jaggery. It is exceedingly hard. To use it, grate the whole block by hand against a cheese grater, or hack a piece off and dissolve it as directed in the recipe.

Papaya

These are also called paw-paw. The ones sold in many supermarkets are normally pear-shaped but two or three times as big as a pear, with green skin when they are still unripe. The skin becomes orangey-yellow when ripe, and soft to the touch. The Thais have a very good salad of green papaya and grated carrots, with a piquant dressing mixed with pounded dried shrimps. Ripe papaya is good for fruit salad (see page 121). To prepare it, cut it in half, scoop out the seeds with a spoon, then peel and slice the orange-coloured, juicy flesh to be mixed in the salad. Imported papaya have to be picked while still green, and they never taste as sweet as those ripe from the tree. Occasionally you can buy large, long papaya imported from Thailand. These are a much sweeter variety.

Passion fruit

I used to have a passion fruit plant climbing up the wall of my garden in Java; we used them to make passion fruit juice. Now, they are becoming widely available in the west. The juice mixed with mango pulp makes a really delicious fool (page 49).

Peanuts – see Nuts

Pineapple

This is particularly good as a dessert fruit because it contains chemical substances that aid digestion. Unripe fruit, indeed, are said to do this to the extent of being violently purgative, but I have known many Javanese, Malaysians and Thais who ate them as part of their chilli-hot fruit salad with no ill-effects. In most supermarkets you find large and medium-sized pineapples from the Ivory Coast, which are very good. Recently small pineapples from Thailand have also become available.

The Thais use these pineapples, among other things, in curries and mix them with fried rice. I have eaten, in a restaurant, a pineapple fried rice served inside a whole pineapple – good to eat as well as to look at.

Poppyseed

The black poppyseeds used in the Poppyseed Parfait (on page 131) are obtainable from the spice counters of supermarkets and delicatessens. They are in fact the seeds of the opium poppy, though they contain no opium; the colour is actually dark blue rather than black.

Prawns, uncooked

In most shops, the only uncooked prawns you can buy are frozen. They are either medium-size or 'king' prawns, and are almost always without heads. These are the ones to use for all the prawn pastes described in this book, and are also stipulated for some other recipes. It is absolutely essential to thaw them completely before cooking – the cooking time is always very short, and if the prawn is still part-frozen inside bacteria may survive the cooking process.

Rice

It is encouraging to see supermarkets now selling six or eight different kinds of rice, and customers learning to discriminate among them. Long-grain rices (e.g. Patna, Basmati) tend to cook drier and with the grains separate, though Thai fragrant and other South-East Asian varieties are stickier, which is what people in those countries prefer. Short-grain rices, grown in Laos, Vietnam, Korea and Japan, tend to be moist and sticky. Some rices are really 'sticky' and are usually labelled glutinous, though they do not contain gluten (which makes rice an ideal food for people with a gluten allergy). Brown rice is usually rice that has been only partly milled and therefore retains some of its coating of bran, which is where most of the nutrients are to be found. White rice, like white bread, is less good for you but more prestigious. Black rice and red rice are just other varieties of rice; black sticky rice is often used for sweets, and in this book I describe a particularly delicious black rice sorbet. Directions for cooking rice will be found on page 25.

Wild rice

This is not really rice, but a distantly-related plant that evolved in lakes and swamps of North America. In fact, most 'wild' rice is now cultivated, but it still grows only in a few places; hence its high price. It looks and tastes nice when mixed with ordinary white rice, but it requires much longer cooking.

Sesame oil

The sesame oil specified here is the Chinese or Japanese variety which is made from roasted sesame seeds. It has a dark yellow colour with a pungent flavour and aroma. I use it, very sparingly, in several of the Burmese and Korean recipes in this book; sometimes it is mixed with vegetable oil. It is too rich for use in deep-frying.

Sesame seed

You can buy these tiny seeds in oriental and health-food shops. There are two kinds, black and white, both used in cooking; in this book, the white ones are used.

Shaohsing wine

A Chinese rice wine, usually sold in square bottles like Johnny Walker bottles. A bit pricey, but worth the money if you want your cooking to have an authentic Chinese flavour. However, dry sherry does make a very fair substitute.

Shiitake mushrooms

What used to be rare Japanese gourmet mushrooms are now almost commonplace, but still delicious. Oriental shops sell dried shiitake, which have to be reconstituted by soaking for 30 minutes in hot water. Fresh ones are available in many supermarkets, most of them grown in Holland. Don't throw away the stalks, which will give flavour to your stock.

Shrimps, dried (also called dried prawns)

You can buy these at most Thai, Malaysian and Chinese shops: packets of tiny shrimps, already shelled, salted and roasted to give them a sharp salt-sweet flavour. They are used either with, or instead of, shrimp paste in making spice mixtures. Before use, they should be soaked in warm water until soft; then they can either be put into the blender, or be pounded in a mortar with a pestle.

Shrimp paste

This is sold in hard blocks or slices, usually labelled *terasi, trassie, balachan* or *blachen*. It is the Indonesian/Malaysian/Burmese equivalent of fish sauce (though the Burmese have a liquid fish sauce as well). It is extremely strong-smelling and extremely salty. Use very sparingly.

Soy sauce

This is fermented from soya beans by a complex process that originated in China at least 2000 years ago. All soy sauces are salty, but they also contain sugar; dark soy contains more sugar than light soy, and tends to give food a darker colour. Chinese shops and many supermarkets sell both kinds. Well-known brands like Amoy and Kikkoman are good for any of the recipes in this book.

Spring roll wrappers

Thin sheets of a kind of pastry; available, usually in three sizes, from most South-East Asian food shops. Like filo pastry, they can be frozen and need to be thawed out and carefully separated before use, but covered with a cloth so they don't dry out.

Tamarind slices

Most Chinese shops sell these, usually in plastic packets so you have no choosing to do. They are not really tamarind at all, but they produce exactly the same effect. There is no need to boil or squeeze them – just put a couple of slices into the pot while cooking. Remember to take them out before the dish comes to table.

Tamarind water

Another of the delicately sour flavourings which most South-East Asian savoury dishes require. It is easily made from a tamarind block – this is how tamarind is usually sold in Asian food stores. Break a piece off the block and squeeze and knead it with your hands in warm water. The water will turn an unattractive colour; the more tamarind you use, the darker it will get. Make sure no solids get into it, or else sieve it before use. It can be kept in the fridge for up to a week.

Taro

This root vegetable is sometimes called *eddo* or *dasheen*. It must be cooked long enough to destroy the calcium oxylate crystals that form in some (not all) varieties. These can taste unpleasantly acrid, or even cause mild inflammation in the mouth and throat. For practical purposes there are two common kinds, a large and a small one. For the taro cake recipe on page 159, use the large one, which is available in Chinese shops and in some supermarkets.

Tempeh

This is another ingenious soya bean product, made in Java and some (by no means all) other parts of Indonesia, not much known elsewhere but becoming quite a well-known health food in North America and Holland. It is a soft cake of cooked beans, held together by a special mould which ferments them, makes them digestible, gives them a mild nutty flavour and actually increases their nutritional value. Tempeh is manufactured by several small firms in Britain and can be bought, frozen, from many good health-food shops.

Tofu

This is a soft, creamy substance slightly resembling junket; it is made from soya bean milk and is very good for you though it has little taste or texture. It does, however, absorb the flavours it is marinated in or cooked with. It can be bought fresh in oriental shops, packed in plastic boxes filled with cold water; in water, it can be refrigerated for several days before it goes off. A British company, Cauldron Foods, makes fresh tofu, which is obtainable either natural or smoked. Japanese 'silken' tofu is packed in sealed containers and keeps for many months provided it is not opened; once opened, it must be eaten within a few days at most. It is not advisable to freeze tofu or tofu dishes, because the texture and flavour will be spoilt.

Turmeric

Turmeric is a rhizome which looks very much like ginger. It is available, fresh, in Chinese and Thai shops, but I suggest you use the ground turmeric which is obtainable from the spice counters in most supermarkets. If you are using fresh turmeric, peel it, then chop or slice it and mix it with other spices in the blender to make a curry paste. Turmeric juice will stain most things, and the stain is practically impossible to remove from cloth.

Water chestnuts

These can be bought in cans, usually labelled Produce of China, at all East Asian shops. They have little flavour but a beautifully crunchy texture, which makes them popular in dishes where they contrast with some other ingredient – e.g. in little canapés consisting of a water chestnut surrounded by a tiny rasher of bacon, pinned by a cocktail stick and roasted for 10 minutes in a medium oven.

Wild rice – see Rice

Wonton skins

Yet another kind of extremely thin pastry, cut up into 7.5-cm (3-inch) squares in Chinese shops. Can be frozen, must be thawed thoroughly before use; don't allow to dry out as this makes them brittle.

Woodears fungus

These dried fungi come from Chinese shops, where they are sold at a high price, though cheaper than dried mushrooms. They appear to be hard, crumpled bits of black bakelite, until soaked in hot water for 30 minutes. They then become leathery, and taste delicious when they have been cooked.

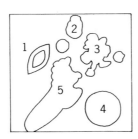

1 Chilli powder
2 Mirin
3 Dried shiitake mushrooms
4 Yellow split muang beans
5 Pak choy

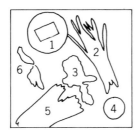

1 Shrimp paste
2 Lemon grass
3 Black fungus
4 Palm sugar
5 Rice sticks
6 Chillies

Yard-long beans

These are green beans, and can actually grow up to a yard long. They should be bought and cooked very fresh, and not over-cooked; like French beans, they should have a crisp, firm texture. If you can find a Thai shop that has fresh vegetables flown in regularly, that is the best place to get them; but many oriental food shops have them, and as long as they look green and flexible you can buy them confidently.

Yellow beans

Chinese shops sell yellow beans and black beans, sometimes loose, sometimes in boxes, sometimes in tins (in which case they are often described as 'in salted sauce'). They are all variations on fermented soya beans, and all are quite delicious when used in accordance with the recipes.

Yellow bean sauce

A variation on the above; the beans have been mashed into a pulp. The sauce is still very flavoursome and very salty.

Yogurt – see Cream

Shopping

THIS BOOK COULD not have been written if new ingredients had not appeared in food shops during the past ten years or so. We must hope that this revolution will continue – I don't think revolution is too strong a word. People are far more enterprising and adventurous in their cooking and eating than they used to be. Because of this, shops keep changing: little ones come and go, big ones stay but are constantly diversifying, adding new lines, discarding others.

Big supermarkets are becoming good non-ethnic places for all-round shopping for the ingredients mentioned in this book. They carry an increasingly wide range of tropical fruits and vegetables, chillies, coriander leaves and other herbs, and of course spices. Their produce is rather highly priced, but it is carefully selected and therefore good value.

Specialist food shops and delicatessens are also good sources of unusual spices and imported fruit and vegetables. Most health food shops sell tofu, many sell tempeh, and nearly all have a choice of rice, spices, pulses and oils.

In areas with large Chinese and Indian populations you will find plenty of ethnic food shops, often run on supermarket lines – it's up to you to look around and find what you need. Customer service and advice may be forthcoming, but staff are generally too busy to talk – or maybe they aren't too confident of their English. As more Thais, Malaysians, Indonesians, Vietnamese and Japanese come to live in the west, they open their own food shops, and the proprietors of these are often extremely helpful. The Thais, in particular, are likely to have fresh produce flown in weekly from Bangkok.

Finally, don't forget street markets for fruit and vegetables. Many in big-city areas have stalls selling exotic greengrocery.

Cooking methods

Cooking Rice

In countries where rice is the staple food, everyone considers himself a connoisseur. To start with, the rice should be the best available. The three types of long-grain rice I normally use are Thai fragrant, also known as Jasmine rice, Basmati and Patna. And of course it should be cooked to perfection. This is easy. If you have an electric rice steamer, you are almost guaranteed perfect results, but you can cook beautiful rice in an ordinary saucepan.

Remember that 2 cups of dry, uncooked rice will absorb a lot of water; this quantity would be enough to feed my family of four adults. We are moderate rice-eaters; the same amount might feed only two hungry Indonesians, or six English people who don't eat rice very often.

It is important to measure the water accurately: always measure rice and water in the same cup. For 2 cups of rice, use 2 cups of water. An extra ¼ or ½ cup of water will make the rice a little softer. But don't add any extra water if you are going to fry the rice afterwards – rice for frying needs to be dry and not too soft. We don't usually add salt to plain cooked rice.

Wash the rice before you cook it: put in the pan, pour enough cold water over it to cover it, swirl it around with your fingers and pour the water away, looking to see that it takes with it any bits of husk or dirt that might have got in. You can repeat this process once or twice if you like. The last time, pour away as much of the water as you easily can – there is no need to squeeze out every last drop.

With an electric rice cooker, all you need do is to put in the rice and the water and switch on the cooker. It will switch off automatically when the rice is done, and you can take it straight to the table.

This is how to cook rice in a saucepan, using 2 cups long-grain rice, white or brown, washed, and 2 cups cold water. Put the rice and the water in the saucepan, put the pan on a medium heat and bring the water to the boil. Stir once with a wooden spoon, and let the rice simmer, uncovered, until all the water has been absorbed. Then . . .

FOUR WAYS TO FINISH COOKING THE RICE

1 The traditional Oriental way is to keep the rice in the same saucepan and cover it tightly. Lower the heat as low as possible, and leave the rice undisturbed for 15–16 minutes. Then put the saucepan on top of a wet tea towel (this is important to prevent the bottom layer from sticking to the pan) placed on your draining board. After 3 minutes, uncover the saucepan and transfer the rice to a serving bowl. Serve it hot, or let it cool if you are going to make fried rice. You will find that a layer of rice about ½ cm (¼ inch) thick will come off the bottom of the saucepan, like a cake from a cake tin. In Indonesia, we call this rice-cake *intip*. Don't throw it away; dry it in the sun, or in the oven, as if you were drying bread for breadcrumbs. When it is dry, break it into small pieces and store in an airtight container. When you have a good quantity, say 1 kg (2¼ lb) or so, deep-fry the pieces in hot oil until they are puffed up and just starting to colour. Sprinkle them with a little salt, and you have an unusual and delicious crisp snack to serve with drinks.

2 If you don't want to save this rice 'cake', transfer the rice from the pan to a steamer and steam for 10 minutes.

3 Another way to finish cooking the rice is to transfer it to an ovenproof dish. Cover the dish with buttered greaseproof paper, then with aluminium foil. Put it in a preheated oven at 180°C/350°F/Gas Mark 5 for 10–12 minutes.

4 Alternatively, transfer the rice to a container which can be microwaved, cover it with clingfilm, set the microwave oven to full power, and cook the rice for 4–5 minutes.

Using Coconut and Coconut Milk

Young green coconuts are hardly ever available outside the tropics, but the 'fresh' ones you buy in supermarkets are usually good; they are brown because their outer husks have been cleaned off before shipping. When you split a coconut and take out the flesh, a brownish rind always comes with it. For most savoury dishes, this can be left on when the flesh is grated, but for delicately-coloured sweets you need to pare off and discard it.

Creamed coconut

This is sold in blocks, like a hard, white margarine. It is very useful for giving flavour and a little thickening in a number of these recipes. It needs to be cut into small pieces – either by chopping with a sharp knife, or shaving thin slices off it. These usually go into the blender with other ingredients.

Desiccated coconut

The familiar white flakes are usually thought of as something to decorate cakes. They are also the next best raw material, after fresh coconut, for making coconut milk for cooking. Familiar supermarket brands are all right for this, but Asian shops usually sell larger packets of unsweetened coconut at much lower prices. Unfortunately it is sometimes kept in stock much too long and starts to taste rancid. If it smells rancid through the plastic bag, don't buy it.

Coconut milk

This is not the liquid that sloshes about inside the nut before you crack it open – that is coconut water, and is only good to drink. The 'milk' is extracted from the grated flesh, and is essential for many dishes in this book. Luckily it is very easy to make. (You can buy ready-made canned coconut milk, and instant powdered coconut milk; both are usable, but they do not have as good a flavour and I would only use them if I had nothing else.)

1   from fresh coconut

One nut makes about 600 ml (1 pint) of milk. Grate the flesh and pour hot water over it; leave till it has cooled somewhat, then press and squeeze it to extract the milk and press it in a fine sieve to get the last drop out. If the recipe specifies thick milk, use less water; for thinner milk, use more.

2   from desiccated coconut

350 g/12 oz desiccated coconut makes 600 ml (1 pint) of thick milk. By repeating the process described below with the same batch of coconut but fresh water, you will get a second extraction of thin milk. By mixing the two, you will get medium milk, which is the 'normal' kind.

With a blender: Put the desiccated coconut into the blender with half the water (fairly hot). Blend for 20–30 seconds, then pass the result through a fine sieve. Put the coconut back into the blender, pour in the rest of the water (fairly hot) and repeat.

Without a blender: Put the desiccated coconut in a pan with the water and simmer for 4–5 minutes. Allow to cool somewhat, then sieve and strain.

Storage and use

The milk must be used fresh; it will keep in the fridge for 48 hours at most. This may cause the thick 'cream' to separate and come to the top – if this happens, just stir it all back together again. Coconut milk cannot be frozen. If cooking for the freezer, omit the coconut milk and only add it when the dish is thawed ready for reheating.

Steaming

One of the cooking methods used in South-East Asia is steaming, and there are quite a number of recipes in this book that call for it. It has advantages – the flavour and goodness of the food are preserved, and it's economical in fuel, which may not matter a great deal in the west but is important if you are cooking over a wood fire.

We steam rice in a rice steamer or double saucepan, and these can also be used to steam little cups or ramekins of savoury food or desserts.

But how would you steam a whole duck or a whole fish if you don't have a very large steamer?

In most recipes where steaming is prescribed I have explained briefly how this is done. However, since I don't want to go into all the details in every recipe, here is a fuller account.

All that is necessary is to provide a platform over a little lake of boiling water, with a lid to keep the steam in. In practice, this usually means using a large-diameter pan. A wok makes an excellent steamer, if you have a domed lid; many wok sets include these, and little wire shelves to support the food, though they are usually on rather a small scale.

The advantage of a saucepan is that it has high sides. Place, in the bottom of it, an upturned soup plate, or a wire trivet, or anything that will remain reasonably firmly in place and will support the platform above the level of the water. The platform is usually another plate or shallow bowl, with the food on it or in it. The water, obviously, must not bubble over the edge of whatever contains the food. At the same time, the pan must not boil dry. The lid should therefore be as tight-fitting as reasonably possible. Some water vapour will still escape, however, and if the steaming goes on for a long time it is obviously wise to check the water level now and then. If it is necessary to add water, this must of course be boiling water straight from the kettle so that the steam continues to surround what is being cooked.

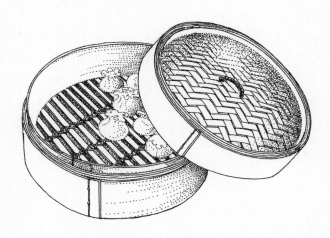

Menus

Winter

WHEN I WAS young, winter was something that happened to other people. The nearest I got to it was a cool breeze blowing on July nights across the sea from Australia. When I first stepped onto European soil with my still quite-new husband, we were in Naples. Late January sunshine warmed the ancient bricks of Pompeii (in those days you could have Pompeii to yourself on a Tuesday morning in January) but sent us rushing to buy thick overcoats. On the steps of St Peter's in Rome a few days later, a German girl behind us breathed deeply and announced to the world at large that spring was really here. I didn't believe her. When we reached London it was freezing, it went on freezing for several weeks and my memories are mainly of radiators, gas fires, coal fires, and slot meters. The winter after that we were in a large, draughty flat in Surrey. Only in my third English winter did I succeed in getting us into a cosy modern flat opposite the Marquis Cornwallis pub in Marchmont Street, London, above a launderette and a Pakistani restaurant. I have never been quite so snug since, but all sorts of things have changed; the Marquis Cornwallis is still there, but the flats were demolished years ago and the climate has started behaving strangely.

I remember the flats of those early years chiefly for the parties we gave in them. How did we ever do so much partying when we had no money? Parties on winter nights especially: the preparatory pleasure of being in the kitchen when it was the only warm room in the building, the unwrapping of guests from their outdoor clothes and parking of carry-cots in the spare bedroom, the bottles of miscellaneous wines that crowded the sideboard and the quantities of steam that billowed through open doors. It was exciting, as time went on, to discover ingredients that I was familiar with at home starting to penetrate into London shops, at first from the Netherlands, then from Malaysia,

Thailand and the Philippines. And in Soho there was more for me to discover from further Asia – China and Japan – than I could easily have found, perhaps, in my own country. I like to think that all those years ago I was already cooking food that had its roots well down into all three cultures: Indonesia, the Far East, Europe. But if I was, then it was an unconscious process. I had no notion then of writing menus or recipes. I only knew that my new English friends enjoyed my cooking, and I wanted to make sure they tasted something new every time they were invited.

At the same time, of course, I was learning a lot about the food of my new home, and the attitudes of people towards it. There was still, in those days, something of the old European carefulness, which I suppose began as a response to the small, uncertain harvests of northern Europe and the long winter when supplies must be hoarded. And some English families seemed very reluctant to eat anything unfamiliar – but that is a common human trait. A neighbour of ours in Marchmont Street told us a touching story about his childhood. His mother had decided one day to make a curry. She misread the directions on the packet of curry powder and put in far, far too much. 'We all came expectantly to the table,' he said. 'We took the first mouthful . . .' he paused and shook his head sadly. 'My father was a fireman. We were a poor family. We had to eat it.' But the experience didn't seem to have left any lasting scars. The boy grew up, survived the war and food rationing, and plainly had a hearty appreciation of foreign food. More important from my point of view, my parents-in-law seemed quite willing to eat what I cooked for them. They and I had had to take each other very much on trust, as I had married an English husband, taken his nationality and sworn allegiance to the Queen, without any first-hand knowledge of where I was going. His mother was, as he had told me, an excellent plain cook, a farmer's daughter who made beautiful pastry and could roast a joint to perfection. These were skills I had not learnt at home, because ovens were rare in Indonesia in those days and were temperamental things, heated by trays of glowing charcoal. I soon added roast beef, Yorkshire pudding and apple pie to the repertoire of European dishes that I had begun to establish before I left Java. Meals with my in-laws were always lavish and enjoyable, though I found it hard to overcome my embarrassment at watching my father-in-law carve, fill plates with meat, and serve each of us, just as if he were not the head of the family.

Looking back, I think I timed my arrival in the West rather well. A new mass market was developing that had the money to experiment in food, clothes, entertainment and holidays, and the will to break away from a past that was seen as narrow and oppressive. On the liner that brought us across the Indian Ocean, my husband said to me: 'We really must find out who the Beatles are – everyone seems to be talking about them.' We all look back on the sixties as a slightly embarrassing golden age of optimistic innocence; so many of those revolutions seemed to end in failure. Some left lasting changes, though – and food was one of them. The change was gradual and is still going on. I suppose a social or economic historian would say that it started long before, when refrigerators and steamships freed these northern lands from seasonal food shortages. Perhaps the real change has been that we can now appreciate and enjoy the seasons – and I have to say that the English cycle of warmth and chill, long days and short days, bud and leaf-fall, does have a charm that is unknown in the moist heat of the tropics, where the sun pops up at 6 am and down at 6 pm every day until the end of the world, and you wait only for the rain either to come or to go away. One of the strangest things I had to get used to in my new home was Christmas, which is a public and religious holiday in Indonesia but quite different in feeling from our great annual feast-day, Hari Raya, Lebaran or Idul Fitri – the end of the Muslim fasting month. I enjoy Christmas much more now as one of the series of great mid-winter feasts – New Year's Eve and Twelfth Night are of course the others – that link our lives with those of pre-Christian Europe, the feasts that mark the turning-point of winter and the recovery of the sun's waning power. From a practical point of view, this must have been the time when you killed and ate the last of the livestock for which there would not be sufficient fodder to last till spring, and gorged yourself stupid because you probably wouldn't see another square meal for months. By the time spring came you would probably be opening the veins of your surviving animals and drinking their blood to give you the strength you had to have to till your fields. Let's be thankful for supermarkets and little ethnic food shops as we meet to celebrate winter.

Dinner for Two

This is a festive dinner for two – I hope that doesn't sound like a contradiction in terms; it isn't meant to, and I don't see why it should. If you're cooking for the same person you sit opposite every night of the year, then this is surely the season to cook that person something really different. If it's a special guest, then at this time of year the food must be really special. Indeed, there are one or two quite expensive ingredients here, but the result is exciting and will be a treat for you and your partner. I have taken into account the fact that you don't want to spend too much time in the kitchen. The recipes are easy and quick to make, and nothing here will spoil your fine wine or champagne.

The Menu

Spicy steamed scallops

◆

Thirty-minute spicy duck
served with
Tagliatelle or Pappardelle
and
Green beans dressed with hot peanut butter

◆

Baked banana with coconut and rum

ABOUT THE FOOD

Spicy steamed scallops

The scallops can be steamed in their shells or in little heatproof dishes or ramekins. My recipe here is not from any particular country, as the dish is made from some of the most widely-used ingredients in Asia. The method of steaming is also widely used all over the area.

Thirty-minute spicy duck

Buy just the breasts of Aylesbury duck (available in large supermarkets), which has a thin skin that will be quite crisp when cooked. (Do not use Barbary duck breasts for this dish, as the skin is too thick to be pleasant to eat.) The marinade for this spicy duck is my Sumatran spice mixture, which is traditionally used to make a really chilli-hot duck stew or casserole.

Tagliatelle or pappardelle

If you don't make your own pasta, buy the real stuff made in Italy, because I know from experience that it is always much better than anything made elsewhere. If you choose tagliatelle, buy the green kind, tagliatelle verde or spinach tagliatelle; if you go for pappardelle, pick the kind that looks beautifully yellow, almost golden. Either type of pasta needs only to be cooked in slightly salted boiling water for 3 to 4 minutes, or a bit less if you want the pasta still to have a little 'bite' left in it.

Green beans dressed with hot peanut butter

For this dish I use the fine French or Kenya beans available in supermarkets; they only need to be washed, and then topped and tailed. If you use larger beans, cut them into two or three pieces. Soaking rather tired-looking beans for 40 minutes in cold water will definitely make them look plumper and nicer. Do this before topping and tailing them.

For this dish, crunchy peanut butter is preferable to the smooth kind.

Baked banana with coconut and rum

Banana, coconut and rum are a perfect combination, though I suppose they suggest Jamaica more than anywhere in the East. The rum for this baked banana can also be poured on at the end of cooking, and flambéed just as the dessert is served.

PLANNING AND PREPARATION

Once you have prepared the bananas, marinated the duck breasts, blanched the beans, cleaned the scallops and prepared the spice mixture, the actual cooking will take almost exactly 30 minutes. Put the duck in the oven, and the scallops in the steamer, 3 minutes before you want to start eating; the scallops take 2 minutes to steam. Start heating a saucepan of water (for the pasta) before you sit down; when you have finished eating the scallops the water will be ready to cook the pasta. By the time you finish tossing the beans in the peanut butter, the duck will be ready as well. Put the prepared bananas into the oven as soon as you've taken out the duck.

The evening before:

Marinate the ducks; store them in the fridge overnight.

On the day:

MORNING

Prepare the bananas, ready to be put into the oven at the last moment. Blanch the beans.
Clean the scallops, and prepare the spice mixture.
All these can be stored in a cool place or in the fridge.

EVENING: For 8 o'clock dinner

7.30   Turn on oven and set to 200°C/400°F/Gas Mark 6.
        Take out of the fridge everything required for the meal.

7.45   Put the duck in the oven to cook.

7.55   Start boiling water in the steamer, and when it is boiling steam the scallops.

8.00   Start heating water for pasta.
        SERVE SCALLOPS

8.10   Cook the pasta, drain and keep warm in a hot serving bowl, covered.
        Mix the beans with peanut butter, transfer to serving dish.

8.15   Take out duck from oven and transfer to dinner plates.
        Turn down oven to 180°C/350°F/Gas Mark 4, and put in banana to cook for 6–8 minutes. It can be left in the oven after 6 minutes cooking, but do not forget to turn the oven off.

Alternatively take the banana out of the oven after 8 minutes, and serve warm or cold.
SERVE THE MAIN COURSE

Spicy Steamed Scallops

If you haven't got a steamer or a double saucepan, steam the scallops in a large saucepan half-filled with boiling water, with a trivet on the bottom for a plate to stand on, above the surface of the water (see page 29). Then you can just put the scallops, in their containers, on the plate. Allow three scallops per person.

6 scallops with corals

For the spice mixture
1 clove garlic, crushed
2 small red chillies, seeded and finely chopped
1 tablespoon chopped Chinese chives, or spring onions
1 tablespoon chopped coriander leaves
1 teaspoon grated ginger (optional)
2 tablespoons fish sauce
1 tablespoon mild vinegar or lemon juice
½ teaspoon sugar

Mix all the ingredients for the spice mixture in a small bowl. Keep in a cool place until needed.

Clean the scallops by removing the black 'beards' and intestines. Put each of them back in its shell, or use two dishes, each large enough to hold three scallops side by side. Pour the spice mixture in equal portions onto the scallops, and steam them for 2 minutes only. Serve immediately.

Thirty-minute Spicy Duck

As explained in the 'planning' section, it is only the cooking that takes 30 minutes. The duck breasts need to be marinated overnight. To enable the marinade to penetrate the duck meat, make two deep cuts with a sharp knife on the skin side of each breast before putting it in the marinade.

2 or 4 Aylesbury duck breasts

For the marinade
4 large green chillies, seeded and chopped
4 shallots, peeled and chopped
2 cloves garlic
4 candlenuts or macadamia nuts, or 5 blanched almonds
a large pinch of turmeric powder
½ teaspoon galingale powder
2.5-cm (1-inch) piece of fresh ginger, peeled and chopped
5-cm (2-inch) stem of lemon grass, outer leaves discarded, the inner part
   then chopped into thin rounds
1 kaffir lime leaf, shredded (optional)
freshly-ground black pepper
½ teaspoon salt
1 tablespoon white malt vinegar
2 tablespoons olive oil

Put all the ingredients for the marinade into a blender, blend them until smooth, and transfer the mixture to a glass bowl. Put in the duck breasts, and turn them over several times to make sure each is well coated with marinade. Cover the bowl with a plate or clingfilm, and keep in the fridge overnight.

Preheat the oven to 200°C/400°F/Gas Mark 6. Drain the marinade from the duck breasts and place them on a rack in a baking tray. Half-fill the tray with hot water and roast in the oven for 30 minutes. Serve immediately.

If you wish, you can make a strong-tasting thick sauce from the marinade, diluting it first, if necessary, with coconut milk or stock. Transfer it to a frying pan and cook, stirring it most of the time, for 20 minutes. This sauce does taste strong, and I find I only need it if I am eating a large quantity of rice with my duck. With this pasta-based menu, you'll find the peanut butter in the beans is sufficient without another strong sauce to compete with it. You can use the left-over marinade to cook other vegetables or potatoes for another meal.

Tagliatelle or Pappardelle

If you are using a packet of dried pasta, follow the cooking instructions on the packet. For home-made pasta, only 2–3 minutes cooking is required.

250–275 g (8–9 oz) tagliatelle verde, or pappardelle
1.25 litres (2 pints) water
½ teaspoon salt
1 tablespoon oil (optional)
1 tablespoon butter (optional)

Boil the water in a large saucepan. When boiling add salt and oil (if used), and the pasta. Keep the water boiling and cook the pasta for 3–4 minutes at most (see above). Drain into a colander, then transfer to a warm serving dish. You can toss the pasta with a little butter if you wish.

Green Beans Dressed with Hot Peanut Butter

225 g (8 oz) green beans, topped and tailed, and, if they are long, cut into 2 or 3 pieces

For the dressing
2 tablespoons crunchy peanut butter
¼ teaspoon Tabasco
1 teaspoon lemon juice
1 tablespoon light soy sauce
1 tablespoon hot water

Mix the dressing ingredients well together in a large serving bowl.

Boil the beans for 4 minutes. Drain off the water and transfer the beans, while they are still hot, to the serving bowl containing the dressing. Mix them thoroughly with the dressing. Serve hot with the main course.

Baked Banana with Coconut and Rum

2–3 medium-size ripe bananas
250 ml (8 fl oz) water
3 tablespoons double cream
1 tablespoon demerara sugar
3 tablespoons desiccated coconut
a pinch of ground cinnamon
1–2 tablespoons dark rum

Peel the bananas and slice them thinly. Mix all the ingredients, except the bananas and rum, in a small saucepan. Simmer them for 4 minutes. Remove them from the heat and add the banana slices and the rum, stirring them in carefully so as not to mash the bananas. Transfer into two well-buttered ramekins or individual-size ovenproof dishes, and bake in the oven at 180°C/350°F/Gas Mark 4 for 6–8 minutes. Serve hot or warm, with more cream poured over them if desired.

A nice alternative is to pour on the rum at the end, just when you've taken out the bananas from the oven, and flambé it as you are sitting down to eat.

Dinner for Six

It occurs to me that this is a very good dinner for vegetarians who eat fish, although I didn't actually have them in mind when I first composed it. I wanted the sort of dinner that would make everyone feel warm and satisfied on a cold, foggy evening, one that would encourage conversation and banish dyspepsia, remind westerners of their roots (chestnuts, pumpkins) and offer them something with quite different associations (yellow rice, mangoes). For easterners, the familiar/unfamiliar contrast may work in just the opposite way.

The Menu

Creamy pumpkin and basil soup

◆

Baked turbot fillets with spices and herbs
served with
Savoury yellow rice
and
Savoy cabbage stuffed with chestnuts

◆

Passion fruit and mango fool

ABOUT THE FOOD

Creamy pumpkin and basil soup

The origin of this is a Thai soup which uses a greenish-purple basil that you can buy in Thai or Indian shops; but sweet basil, which you can either grow in a pot, or buy in most high-street greengrocers or supermarkets, will do very well. The Thais use thick coconut cream, which is very good with pumpkin, and they cut the pumpkin into big chunks. The recipe that I give here still uses coconut milk but the ingredients are all liquidised together into a creamy golden soup.

Baked turbot fillets with spices and herbs

This is an alternative to cooking fish in the Sumatran style, by wrapping it in banana leaves and putting it on charcoal or a wood fire. We normally cook fish whole, and you can of course cook a whole turbot this way, but the fillets are much more manageable. Usually I substitute aluminium foil for the banana leaves, but on this occasion I adopt the western style of cooking *en papillote* so that all the guests can open their 'parcels' at the table and enjoy the fragrance of the spices and herbs.

Savoury yellow rice

Yellow rice is always associated with festivals in the East, so you will find it at any celebration in most parts of South-East Asia. This version is from Indonesia. It can be cooked with coconut milk or stock, and the yellow colour is from turmeric, not saffron.

Savoy cabbage stuffed with chestnuts

Savoy cabbage and chestnuts are very seasonal foods. In this recipe I have combined them with some oriental ingredients and presented them in a form that will not only create a lot of interest at a dinner party but will also give a quite ordinary cabbage an unusual taste.

Passion fruit and mango fool

My friend, the cookery writer Alice Wooledge Salmon, would call this 'a fool which is not so foolish', and I can confidently assert that this fool will attract numbers of passionate fans.

PLANNING AND PREPARATION

For this menu the yellow rice needs to be cooked at the last moment. The fish can be prepared in the morning, and cooked in the oven at the last moment. The soup, cabbage and fool can also be prepared early in the morning on the day of the dinner.

On the day:

MORNING or AFTERNOON
Make mango fool and keep in the fridge until required.
Prepare the stock and the pumpkin. Or you can finish cooking the soup now to be reheated later.
Prepare the fish and keep the parcels in the fridge.
Prepare the stuffed cabbage (this won't take more than 20 minutes) ready to be steamed in the evening.
Keep all these in a cool place or in the fridge.

EVENING, for 8 o'clock dinner
7.10   Take everything required, except mango fool, out of the fridge.

7.20   Start steaming the stuffed cabbage.
        Turn on oven to 180°C/350°F/Gas Mark 4.
        Assemble and finish cooking the soup if not already done in the
        morning.
7.30   Cook the rice.
        Put fish in the oven.
8.00   SERVE THE SOUP
8.15   SERVE THE MAIN COURSE

Creamy Pumpkin and Basil Soup

Pumpkin and sweet basil go excellently together. I have tried several
versions, and this one is the easiest to make. Use either a whole small
pumpkin or a segment of a large one. You can use creamed coconut for
this, or a combination of single cream and creamy Greek yogurt.

1 kg (2 lb) peeled pumpkin, cut into 2.5-cm (1-inch) cubes

For the stock
1.25 litres (2 pints) water
1 small onion
5-cm (2-inch) piece of lemon grass
2.5-cm (1-inch) piece of fresh galingale, peeled
6 sweet basil leaves
½ teaspoon salt

To be added later
125 g (4 oz) creamed coconut, or 100 ml (3 fl oz) single cream and 100 ml
    (3 fl oz) Greek yogurt
¼ teaspoon ground white pepper
1 tablespoon fish sauce

For the garnish
more sweet basil, whole leaves or chopped

Bring the ingredients for the stock to the boil, then simmer for 30
minutes. Then strain the stock into another saucepan.
    Add the pumpkin cubes and cook for 8 minutes. Add the creamed
coconut, or single cream and yogurt, and stir until it has all dissolved.
Continue to simmer for 2 more minutes, then add the white pepper and

fish sauce, and taste. Put the whole thing into a liquidiser and blend until smooth and creamy. Up to this point the soup can be made in the morning. Keep refrigerated until needed. Reheat in a saucepan. Bring slowly to the boil, then cook, stirring the soup all the time, for 3 minutes. Adjust the seasoning and serve piping hot with some chopped or whole basil sprinkled on top as a garnish.

Baked Turbot Fillets with Spices and Herbs

You need 6 sheets of greaseproof paper, each 25 × 38 cm (10 × 15 inches). Fold each sheet of paper in half and cut into a half-moon shape with the fold in the middle. Brush one side of the paper with butter or oil. Keep aside while preparing the fish and spices.

6 fillets of turbot, weighing about 175 g (6 oz) each
2 tablespoons tamarind water or juice of 1 lime
1 teaspoon salt
½ teaspoon chilli powder

For the spice mixture
4 shallots, chopped
3 cloves garlic, chopped
4 candlenuts (optional)
2–4 large red chillies, seeded and chopped
2.5-cm (1-inch) piece of lemon grass, chopped
2 kaffir lime leaves
300 ml (½ pint) very thick coconut milk
1 teaspoon ground coriander
a pinch of galingale powder
¼ teaspoon turmeric powder
salt to taste
3 tablespoons chopped mint or basil
6 spring onions, cut into thin rounds

Rub the fish fillets all over with the tamarind water (or lime juice), salt and chilli powder, and leave the fish in a cool place while preparing the rest of the ingredients.

Put the shallots, garlic, candlenuts (if used), chillies, lemon grass and kaffir lime leaves in a blender with 4 tablespoons of the coconut milk, and blend to a smooth paste. Put the paste in a saucepan, bring to the boil, stir and add the ground coriander, galingale powder, turmeric powder and salt. Pour in the rest of the coconut milk and simmer until reduced by half. Adjust seasoning and leave to cool.

Lay the circular sheets of paper flat on the table, oiled side up, and put one fish fillet on one half of each sheet. Divide the thick sauce equally among them, and sprinkle each fillet with its fair share of the chopped mint or basil and spring onions. Fold the paper over, and seal the parcels by folding the edges tightly together. (At this point you can store the parcels in the fridge for several hours.)

Place the parcels on a baking tray and bake in the oven at 180°C/ 350°F/Gas Mark 4 for 15–20 minutes. Serve immediately.

Savoury Yellow Rice

Yellow rice is always considered to be festival food, for family celebrations as well as for offering to gods in the temples. For this recipe the rice should be soaked in cold water for 1 hour.

500 g (1 lb) long-grain rice, such as Basmati, Thai fragrant or Patna
2 tablespoons vegetable oil
3 shallots, finely sliced
1 teaspoon turmeric powder
1 teaspoon ground coriander
½ teaspoon ground cumin
600 ml (1 pint) coconut milk or stock
1 stick cinnamon
2 cloves
½ teaspoon salt
1 kaffir lime leaf or bay leaf

Soak the rice for 1 hour, wash, and drain. Heat the oil in a saucepan and fry the sliced shallots, stirring all the time, for 2 minutes. Add the rice, turmeric, coriander and cumin, stir-fry for another 2 minutes, and then put in the coconut milk or stock and the other ingredients. Boil the mixture, uncovered, stirring it once or twice with a wooden spoon, until the liquid has been soaked up by the rice. Then steam for 10 minutes. Alternatively, just cover the saucepan tightly and leave on a low heat, undisturbed, for 10 minutes; or finish cooking in the oven, in a shallow bowl, covered with aluminium foil, for 15 minutes, or in a suitable bowl in the microwave, covered with clingfilm, on full power, for 4–5 minutes. Serve hot.

Savoy Cabbage Stuffed with Chestnuts

This, when it comes to table, will look like a complete cabbage, until you cut into it and reveal the chestnut stuffing speckled with red peppers. The hotness of the stuffing can be as strong or as mild as you like; it depends entirely on how many chillies you use.

a whole Savoy cabbage, 1.25–1.50 kg (3–3½ lb)
500 g (1 lb) fresh or unsweetened canned chestnuts
3 tablespoons groundnut or olive oil
4 shallots, finely sliced
3 cloves garlic, finely sliced
2–6 red chillies, seeded and finely sliced
1 teaspoon ground coriander
½ teaspoon ground white pepper
2 tablespoons desiccated coconut
150 ml (¼ pint) hot water
½ teaspoon salt
2 red peppers, blanched, seeded and skinned, then diced

Separate the outer leaves of the cabbage, and trim the hard stalks from each leaf. Boil these outer leaves in slightly salted water for 8 minutes. Drain in a colander. Shred the heart of the cabbage finely and keep aside.

If fresh chestnuts are used, boil them for 4 minutes, then peel and chop them roughly. Canned chestnuts need only be drained and chopped roughly.

Heat the oil in a wok or large frying pan and fry the shallots, garlic and chillies, stirring all the time, for 2 minutes. Add the shredded heart of the cabbage, continue stir-frying for 2 minutes, then add the rest of the ingredients except the diced red pepper and chopped chestnuts. Stir and let this simmer, covered, for 3–4 minutes. Uncover the wok/pan, add the red pepper and chestnuts, and stir continuously for 1 minute. Adjust the seasoning.

Line a large round heatproof bowl with some of the blanched outer leaves of the cabbage, arranging them upside down so that they will be right way up when, eventually, the stuffed cabbage is turned out onto the serving dish. Put in the stuffing. Press the stuffing down slightly with a spoon. Continue adding more of the outer leaves, finally closing them over the stuffing so that the whole shape of the cabbage is reconstructed in the bowl.

Cover the bowl with aluminium foil. Put the covered bowl in a steamer, and steam for 40 minutes. Alternatively, put the bowl in a large saucepan, pour in hot water so that it comes up to about the halfway mark on the outside of the bowl, cover the saucepan and cook, keeping the water boiling, for 30 minutes.

To serve: Discard the aluminium foil, lay a large serving plate upside-down on top of the bowl, then turn the whole thing over, and lift off the bowl. Bring the cabbage to table whole, then cut it in half with a large, sharp knife, and cut each half into three.

Passion Fruit and Mango Fool

Although they are still quite expensive, mangoes are plentiful – mainly imported from Puerto Rico. It is a pity we never get the Indonesian or the Manila mangoes here; for me they are the best-tasting, juicy and sweet and not at all stringy. Passion fruit are also easily available at this time of the year. Choose the ones with wrinkled skins, they are very ripe and not too sour and have a beautiful scent.

   2 ripe mangoes, peeled
   8 ripe passion fruit, cut in halves
   3 tablespoons caster sugar
   juice of one small lemon
   250 ml (8 fl oz) double cream

Cut up the mango flesh and put it in a liquidiser. Scoop out the passion fruit seeds with the juice and strain through a sieve into the liquidiser. Discard the seeds. Add the sugar and lemon juice and liquidise the whole thing for a few seconds.

Whip the cream until it stands in peaks, and add this to the liquidiser with the mango and passion fruit purée. Turn the liquidiser on for 2 seconds or until the cream is well mixed with the fruit purée. Divide the mixture equally into 6 stemmed glasses, and chill until needed. For best results chill the fool for at least 4 hours but not longer than 24 hours.

Buffet Party for Fourteen to Sixteen

This is designed to be a straightforward, no-hassle job for the single-handed cook. I don't pretend it can be done in 30 minutes flat, but it does not take unreasonably long, you never need to be doing too many things at a time, and you will end up attending and enjoying your own party. This menu I have always found very successful on those post-Christmas occasions when most of us feel like getting away from traditional food and certainly don't want anything that reminds us of the leftovers in the fridge at home. It is also ideal for vegetarians, since there is only one meat dish – the duck – in the entire menu, and the other dishes are satisfying and nourishing even without this. It is also a menu which gives you almost unlimited scope for adding your own green salads.

The Menu

Filo pastry with mushroom filling
and/or
Mushrooms stuffed with lentils and cheese

◆

Savoury sweetcorn cakes
and/or
Savoury potato cakes

◆

Long-cooked Balinese duck
Curried cauliflower gratin
Spiced rice salad

◆

Anne Willan's chocolate hazelnut cake

ABOUT THE FOOD

Filo pastry with mushroom filling

The idea for this recipe is a spicy Javanese mushroom packet (wrapped in banana leaves, naturally) which is sold by street vendors all over Central Java. I remember well the ones I used to buy during my student days at the crossroads near the university campus in Yogyakarta. They were delicious. I haven't managed to get exactly the identical taste in mine, and I blame this on the mushrooms, which are not the same kind. In Java they always use very fresh home-grown straw mushrooms. With wild or field mushrooms in Europe, this recipe comes very close indeed to its original. Here, however, for a large party I suggest using ordinary button mushrooms and making them into a pie, which you can cut into squares.

Mushrooms stuffed with lentils and cottage cheese

If you think your guests will prefer the creaminess of cheese to the coconut cream used in the Javanese mushroom recipe (above), try this one. The idea came from a Burmese recipe for red lentil soup which a friend gave me. The water for the soup is only added after the lentils are cooked, and I found the consistency and the taste of the lentils so good without the water that it seemed a shame to dilute them. With the addition of cottage cheese, these stuffed mushrooms become a dish that will be popular at any party.

Savoury sweetcorn cakes

These little cakes or fritters (the recipe here is from Thailand, but they are basically the same everywhere) can be as bland or as savoury as you wish. When I was little, they were staple food for children, a standard treat because they were different from the plain corn-on-the-cob that everybody ate in the street. Values get strangely reversed as one travels. I am not really sure whether, in England, corn-on-the-cob isn't considered a more sophisticated party food than corn fritters, at any rate for adults. But I remember how popular the fritters were when I had my shop; on Saturday mornings I was in the kitchen making them as hard as I could go. They are good even when cold, and when hot are absolutely irresistible.

Savoury potato cakes

The same is true of these: this is one of many variants on a multi-national basic recipe. You can make plenty of these in advance, they will heat up very nicely in the oven.

Long-cooked Balinese duck

In Bali, a duck is usually stuffed with green vegetables and cooked (in a trench) for up to 12 hours. The result, though it tastes superb, isn't much to look at: just a mass of soft, very dark-looking meat. I wouldn't cook any Balinese duck of mine, if it was a whole bird, longer than 4 hours (in a fan-assisted oven). This version uses the breast meat only and is cooked for 3 hours at most. It is very aromatic and delicious and also very practical, because you can just leave it undisturbed for the whole cooking time while you are busy with other things.

Curried cauliflower gratin

The name speaks for itself: heating this curry in the oven as a gratin makes it almost a convenience food. You will also find that even those of your guests who usually avoid curry will take to this one quite easily.

Spiced rice salad

I don't remember having a rice salad in South-East Asia, except in restaurants in big international hotels where they serve a lot of East-meets-West dishes. This must be because we only use the word 'salad' for dishes that actually use salad leaves and raw vegetables and fruit, and no one ever thinks of making rice salad even under another name. But here is one; I remember making it for the first time, not in winter but on a camping trip to Italy, with fresh local ingredients but, for some reason, boil-in-the-bag rice.

Chocolate hazelnut cake

This is another borrowed recipe, this time from Anne Willan's *Real Food*, published by Macmillan. I have made this cake myself many, many times and it has never let me down once. Incidentally, as it has no flour, it is an ideal cake for anyone with a gluten allergy.

PLANNING AND PREPARATION

Ideally the advance preparation of this menu is done on the previous day, and the chocolate hazelnut cake can be done two days ahead if you wish. With the cake already out of the way, you can be quite relaxed on the day before and the day of the party.

Two days before:

Make the chocolate hazelnut cakes. Keep in a cake box or plastic box with airtight lid in a cool place or fridge.

The day before:

Prepare and cook the filo pastry with mushroom filling. Keep in the fridge, well covered, until required. This is to be reheated for serving warm. It can also be served cold; keep at room temperature for 30 minutes prior to serving.

Marinate the ducks and keep in the fridge until required.

Prepare and cook the potato cakes to be reheated in the oven in the evening.

On the day:

MORNING

Prepare the batter for the sweetcorn cakes. Keep in the fridge until you are ready to fry the cakes in the evening.

Make the rice salad; keep in the fridge until 20 minutes before serving.

Prepare and cook the cauliflower ready for last-minute cooking in the oven.

Prepare the mushrooms and lentil and cheese filling.

AFTERNOON

4.00   Take the ducks out of the fridge. Turn on oven to 160°C/325°F/ Gas Mark 3.

4.10   Put ducks in the oven to cook.

5.10   Turn down oven to 120°C/250°F/Gas Mark ½.
        Fry the sweetcorn cakes (to be served at room temperature).

EVENING – for 7.30 dinner

6.45   Take everything from the fridge that is required.
        Take out the ducks from the oven and turn up the oven to 180°C/350°F/Gas Mark 4.

7.00   Put the cauliflower gratin in the oven.

7.05   Put the mushrooms with lentil and cheese filling in the oven.

7.20   Put the potato cakes in the oven.
       Slice the ducks and arrange on a hot serving platter, ready to
       serve.

7.30   Arrange everything on the table.
       DINNER IS SERVED

Filo Pastry with Mushroom Filling

You will need a 425-g (14-oz) packet of filo pastry, which is obtainable, frozen, from most supermarkets; also two non-stick Swiss roll tins, each about 22.5 × 32.5 cm (9 × 13 inches).

3 tablespoons groundnut oil
8 shallots or 2 onions, chopped
3 cloves garlic, chopped
3 large green chillies, seeded and finely sliced
1 teaspoon finely-chopped ginger
1 teaspoon shrimp paste or anchovy paste
1 kg (2 lb) mushrooms, sliced
75 g (3 oz) creamed coconut, cut into small pieces
6 tablespoons water
3 tablespoons chopped parsley
salt to taste
2 eggs
75 g (3 oz) butter, melted
425-g (14-oz) packet of filo pastry, thawed

Heat the oil in a large frying pan. Add the shallots or onions and fry until they are transparent. Add the garlic, chillies, ginger and shrimp or anchovy paste, stir for 1 minute, then add the mushrooms and cook over a high heat for 6 minutes, stirring occasionally. Add the creamed coconut and water, continue cooking for 2 more minutes. Remove from heat, leave to cool to room temperature, then mix in the parsley, salt to taste and the eggs.

With the butter, brush the inside of two 22.5 × 32.5 cm (9 × 13 inch) non-stick Swiss roll tins. Line each tin with 4 to 6 of the filo

1 Tamarind pulp
2 Turmeric
3 Kaffir lime leaf
4 Dry bean curd
5 Kaffir lime
6 Papaya

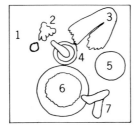

1 Fish sauce
2 Purple basil
3 Rice vermicelli
4 Paprika
5 Tamarind water
6 Wild rice
7 Galingale

sheets, making sure that some of them overlap the edges of the tin, and brushing butter between each layer.

Divide the mushroom mixture in two equal portions and spread it over the pastry, smoothing it down with the back of a spoon. Fold in the overlapping filo sheets, and cover with the remaining sheets, brushing them with butter as before. Score the top of each filo cake with a sharp-pointed knife into 8 or 16 portions. Brush with butter, and cook in a preheated oven at 190°C/375°F/Gas Mark 5 for 25–30 minutes.

Mushrooms Stuffed with Lentils and Cottage Cheese

Choose large cup mushrooms, about 2.5–4 cm (1–1¼ inches) in diameter so that you can put plenty of stuffing on them. They look particularly good if you put the cheese mixture on the left and the lentil mixture on the right, so that you have two half-circles of different colours.

28–32 mushrooms, wiped clean and the stalks removed

For the lentil stuffing
250 g (8 oz) red lentils, soaked for 1 hour and drained
3 tablespoons sesame or olive oil
5-cm (2-inch) piece of lemon grass, outer leaves discarded and the soft
    inner part finely chopped
1 teaspoon finely-chopped ginger
3 cloves garlic, finely chopped
¼ teaspoon chilli powder
a large pinch of turmeric
125 ml (4 fl oz) water
salt to taste

For the cottage cheese filling
250 g (8 oz) cottage cheese
2 tablespoons chopped Chinese chives, or the green part of spring onions
salt and pepper to taste

Heat the sesame or olive oil in a wok or a large frying pan and in it fry the other ingredients (except the lentils, water and salt) for a minute or so, then add the lentils, stir, add the water, and simmer for 4–5 minutes, stirring often. Season with salt to taste, and leave to cool.

Mix all the ingredients for the cottage cheese stuffing in a bowl. When the lentil stuffing is cold, start stuffing the mushrooms, putting lentils on the right of each mushroom and cottage cheese on the left. Place the stuffed mushrooms on a well-greased shallow heatproof dish, and bake in the oven at 180°C/350°F/Gas Mark 4 for 25–30 minutes. Serve hot or cold.

Savoury Sweetcorn Cakes

Although these little cakes or fritters are very good for snacks or picnics, they are equally good with, or instead of, rice, potatoes or pasta. In this menu your guests can choose, but for a buffet party like this, do allow at least two cakes per person.

3 375-g (12-oz) cans of sweetcorn, drained
2 shallots, finely chopped
2 cloves garlic, finely chopped
½ teaspoon ground cumin
1 teaspoon ground coriander
a large pinch turmeric powder
¼ teaspoon chilli powder
1–2 eggs
6 tablespoons rice flour or wheat flour
salt and pepper to taste
some corn or sunflower oil for shallow frying

Put the drained sweetcorn in a large bowl, and mash it a little with a potato masher to break up the kernels so that they won't pop when fried. Mix in the rest of the ingredients. The mixture can be fried straight away or left to stand for 30 minutes to 1 hour (maximum).

Put about ½ cm (¼ inch or less) of oil in a frying pan and heat it. Put a tablespoonful of the mixture into the pan, pressing it lightly to make a flat, small cake; repeat this until the pan is full. You will probably be able to fry about 5 or 6 cakes at a time. Fry them for about 2 minutes, then turn them over and continue cooking for another 2 minutes. Remove the cakes with a slotted spoon onto a plate lined with absorbent paper.

If you are frying these sweetcorn cakes in advance, keep them in the fridge, and heat them in a medium oven, in a single layer on a baking tray, for about 8 minutes. They can be served hot, warm or cold.

Savoury Potato Cakes

These cakes can be made either with or without minced beef. Either way, you will get a better result if they are deep-fried in a wok or a deep fryer.

500 g (1 lb) potatoes, preferably a floury kind (e.g. King Edward, Maris Piper; or I usually use Desirée)
2 tablespoons vegetable oil
1 large onion, finely chopped
250 g (8 oz) lean minced beef (optional)
¼ teaspoon freshly-ground black pepper
¼ teaspoon grated nutmeg
2 egg yolks, lightly beaten
salt to taste
2 egg whites, lightly beaten
vegetable oil for deep frying

Boil the potatoes in their skins until cooked; leave them to cool a little, then peel them. Put the peeled potatoes in a large bowl and mash them until smooth.

Put the 2 tablespoons of oil in a wok or frying pan, and fry the onion until transparent, then add the minced beef, pepper and nutmeg. Stir, and continue cooking, stirring occasionally, for 4 minutes. Then take the pan off the heat and let the mixture cool. When cool, mix it with the mashed potatoes. Add the egg yolks, mix well and adjust the seasoning. Up to this point the mixture can be prepared well in advance. Keep in a cool place or in the fridge.

When you are ready to deep-fry the potato cakes, form the mashed-potato mixture into a ball the size of a walnut, flatten it between the palms of your hands, and put in on a tray. Continue making the cakes until all the mixture is used up.

Heat the oil in a wok or a deep-fryer, dip each cake in the egg white, and fry, 5 or 6 at a time, until they are golden brown. Serve hot or cold.

Long-cooked Balinese Duck

In Bali you would cook a whole duck, but here, as an alternative, we use only the breast fillet. These are sold, packaged together in pairs, in most supermarkets. The duck breasts are marinated overnight, and cooked in the oven for 2–3 hours, without the trouble of basting them.

14–16 duck breast fillets

For the marinade
6 shallots, chopped
4 cloves of garlic, chopped
3 red chillies, seeded and chopped, or 1 teaspoon chilli powder
5 candlenuts or 8 blanched almonds, chopped
3 teaspoons coriander seed
¼ teaspoon ground or grated nutmeg
½ teaspoon ground cinnamon
1 teaspoon salt
2 tablespoons lime or lemon juice
3 tablespoons olive oil
2 tablespoons water

Put all the ingredients for the marinade in a blender or food processor, and blend them to a smooth paste. Transfer the paste to a wok or a saucepan, bring it to the boil, then cook, stirring all the time, for 4–5 minutes or until the smell of raw shallots and garlic has been replaced by a pleasant spicy fragrance. Leave to cool.

When the paste is cool, mix it with the duck in a bowl. Everything up to this point can be done the day before, and the duck breasts can then be left in the fridge overnight so that the meat marinates thoroughly.

To cook, preheat the oven to 160°C/325°F/Gas Mark 3, arrange the duck breasts side by side on a baking tray, and cook them, loosely covered, for 2–3 hours, turning the oven down to 120°C/250°F/Gas Mark ½ after the first hour, and removing the cover during the last 30 minutes of cooking.

To serve: slice the duck breasts thinly and arrange them on a large serving dish for your guests to help themselves.

Curried Cauliflower Gratin

To make enough for 14–16 people you need 2–3 large cauliflowers, and two gratin dishes, each measuring about 22.5 cm (9 inches) square.

2–3 large cauliflowers, divided into small florets, blanched

For the curry paste
3 tablespoons groundnut or olive oil
3 shallots, finely sliced
2 cloves garlic, chopped
2 large red or green chillies, seeded and chopped
2 green cardamoms
1 teaspoon ground coriander
½ teaspoon ground cumin
½ teaspoon turmeric

Other ingredients
3 tablespoons natural yogurt
125 g (4 oz) desiccated coconut
150 ml (¼ pint) water
2 tablespoons chopped parsley or coriander leaves
salt to taste

Put all the ingredients for the paste into a blender or food processor, and blend until smooth. Transfer into a saucepan and cook, stirring all the time, for 3–4 minutes. Add the other ingredients, except the chopped parsley or coriander leaves. Stir and simmer for 3 minutes.

Season with salt to taste, then put in the chopped parsley or coriander leaves. Remove half of this coconut mixture into a bowl, and put the cauliflower florets into the saucepan. Continue cooking, stirring most of the time, for 2 more minutes.

Divide the cauliflower florets between two well-greased gratin dishes. Spread the coconut mixture from the bowl equally on top of the cauliflower in each dish, and bake in the oven at 150°C/300°F/Gas Mark 2 for 25–30 minutes. Serve hot or cold.

Spiced Rice Salad

Do not choose pre-cooked or 'easy-cook' rice, even for a rice salad. Use Basmati or other long-grain rice. Soak the rice in cold water for at least 30 minutes. This is the only way to ensure that the rice grains will remain separate when cooked, and for a rice salad separate grains are much to be preferred to the soft and sticky rice that we like in the East.

1 kg (2 lb) Basmati or Patna rice, soaked in cold water for 30–60 minutes, then drained
1.5 litres (2½ pints) water
¼ teaspoon salt
1 tablespoon groundnut or olive oil

Other ingredients
2 tablespoons groundnut or olive oil
2 shallots, finely sliced
2 cloves garlic, finely sliced
2 red chillies, seeded and finely sliced, or ½ teaspoon chilli powder
1 red pepper, seeded and diced
1 aubergine or 2 courgettes, diced
1–2 tablespoons white wine vinegar
salt and pepper to taste

Boil the water in a large saucepan, then add the rice, salt and oil, stir, and quickly bring the water back to the boil. Cook the rice at a rolling boil for 6 minutes. Drain it, and keep aside while you prepare the rest of the ingredients.

Heat the 2 tablespoons of oil in a large frying pan, and fry the shallots, garlic and chillies for 2 minutes, stirring all the time. Add the rest of the ingredients, except the vinegar, and continue stir-frying for 2 minutes. Add the vinegar and salt and pepper, cover the pan, and let it simmer for 3 more minutes. Uncover, and add the rice. Stir and mix well. Adjust seasoning and turn off the heat. Leave the rice to cool to room temperature, then chill until needed.

Chocolate Hazelnut Cake

This recipe is from Anne Willan's book, *Real Food*. She suggests that these quantities will be sufficient for 8 people, and I have found this pretty accurate. So, for a party of 14 to 16 people, you need 2 cakes. To test the cake insert a cocktail stick into the middle of the cake. If it is clean when it comes out, the cake is done. You will need a 20-cm (8-inch) springform cake tin.

For 1 cake
250 g (8 oz) hazelnuts, toasted
220 g (7 oz) unsweetened chocolate
250 g (8 oz) unsalted butter
200 g (6½ oz) sugar
4 eggs, separated
icing sugar (for sprinkling)
vanilla ice cream (for serving)

Butter the tin, line the bottom with greaseproof paper and butter the paper. Heat the oven to 150°C/300°F/Gas Mark 2.

Grind the hazelnuts with the chocolate in two batches in a food processor, or a little at a time in a blender. Alternatively, grind the nuts and chocolate separately with a rotary cheese grater, then mix them.

Cream the butter, add three-quarters of the sugar, and beat until fluffy and light. Beat in the egg yolks, then stir in the chocolate mixture. Stiffly whip the egg whites, add the reserved sugar, and continue whipping for about 30 seconds to make a meringue. Fold the meringue into the hazelnut mixture in three batches.

Spoon the batter into the prepared tin and smooth the top. Bake until the cake tests done: 40–50 minutes. Let it cool in the tin, then run a knife around the edge and remove the side. (Note: The cake is delicate and must be handled gently. You may prefer to serve it from the base of the tin.) It can be stored in an airtight container for up to a week, or frozen.

Just before serving, sprinkle the cake with icing sugar. Serve, with the ice cream in a separate serving dish.

Spring

SPRING FOR ME means gardens: not the kind you sit gracefully in, sipping iced tea, but the kind where you try to scrape the mud from your spade with the sole of your boot, feel a bitter March wind whipping around your knees and ears and marvel at the sheer relentlessness of nature. In my town house, I miss the garden I used to have, but I remember how, in the week after Christmas, I saw small green things begin to appear and realised the winter holidays were over. I remember my next-door neighbour standing with his hands in his pockets, contentedly watching me grub up the roots of some persistent weed. 'It just never stops, does it?' he said, with what I think was meant to be sympathy. I thought of asking him what would happen to us if 'it' ever did stop, but by that time he had gone back indoors.

While I was writing my first book, for Faber, I invited my editor and a colleague to dinner. It was a pleasant evening in late spring, and as soon as the guests arrived they asked to be shown the garden. They were responsible for Faber's gardening list as well as the cookery list and they probably hoped to spot some new talent. We walked around the rather bumpy triangle behind the house – it was really the corner of a field in which a speculative builder of the fifties had strung a loop of little houses and bungalows for the commuter trade; he had left the line of trees at the edge of the field, which had grown from seedlings that survived because the farmer never ploughed right up to the boundary. Those beech trees and sweet chestnuts were the real glory of the garden. Nothing much else flourished in the mixture of wet sand and gravel that the house stood on, though I did grow huge gluts of courgettes among the gladioli. There was also a vine that produced leaves for making dolmas. My Faber guests looked at everything, sighed politely and said: 'Well, you're not really gardeners, are you?' Fortunately the dinner was much more to their taste and we became very good friends; in fact, I owe a lot to their sympathetic encouragement of my first steps as a cookery writer.

My spring menus are all for quite small parties (though of course you can always multiply the quantities and feed a whole wedding reception, if you need to or want to). I am particularly proud of the second menu because to produce a vegan dinner that even meat-eaters will regard as a gastronomic treat does take a little ingenuity. This notion of lavishing thought and care, not to mention money, on an intimate gathering for two or three couples is something I had to learn, because I was never brought up to it. I think my parents perhaps gave little dinner parties in their prosperous days before the war, when we lived in Sumatra, but I was much too small to take any interest. My sisters today, in Jakarta and Pontianak and elsewhere, are adopting a lot of western ways, and even at this distance I can see these reflected in the magazines they send me, particularly the well-established and often excellent cooking-and-entertaining monthly, *Selera* (which means 'Taste'). But the Indonesian instinct, bred by centuries of harvest festivals and village weddings, is always to entertain big, and a middle-class Jakarta dinner party is still a buffet with at least a dozen or twenty guests. Great fun, and socially valuable in a community of large, interlocking circles of family, friends, acquaintances and business contacts, where count is kept of obligations owed and discharged. It's a very different atmosphere, though, from that of an English or American dinner party. The conventions of conversation are quite different, and it is still the custom for men and women to gather in separate groups, something an English hostess tries desperately to prevent. I don't enjoy conversations where people just try to score points at each other's expense, but I like a little cut and thrust around a dinner table and it's fun when guests show a little more of their real selves (and sometimes make better jokes) than they do in everyday life. So, small dinner parties for me – with an occasional big one, just for fun – and may the food, wine and company always be, as we say, *cocok* (pronounced 'tjotjok') – that is, agreeing well together, though not all sounding the same note.

Dinner for Four

This has turned out to be an especially wide-ranging menu: France, China, Thailand, have all contributed. I don't want to sound too complacent, but I can't help thinking it would make rather a good *table d'hôte* menu for a restaurant. I am sure it would appeal equally to businessmen entertaining their clients, two friendly couples celebrating their engagements, or a family of four congratulating one of their number on a new job. It makes a good celebration meal, without being a blow-out.

The Menu

Smoked tofu and asparagus soufflé

◆

Halibut in ginger, garlic and yellow bean sauce
or
Grilled caramelised monkfish fillets
served with
Savoury fried noodles
and
Braised bamboo shoots

◆

Coconut cream brûlé
or
Compôte of rose-scented rhubarb

ABOUT THE FOOD

Smoked tofu and asparagus soufflé

This is another of my experiments in mingling East and West, and very successful it is. The beautiful spring asparagus blends well in taste and texture with the smoked tofu.

Halibut in ginger, garlic and yellow bean sauce

The yellow bean sauce, sometimes labelled 'fermented yellow beans', is available in Chinese and other oriental shops in cans and jars. If it is labelled 'sauce', then the beans are already processed until smooth; otherwise they are still whole and you will need to liquidise them before adding them to the other ingredients. Yellow beans are Chinese in origin, but they are used a lot in other countries as well.

Grilled caramelised monkfish fillets

This is a Thai way of grilling fish out of doors, and you will get the very best results if you grill the fish on a charcoal barbecue. But you don't need to wait for the summer to make this dish; the gas or electric grill in your kitchen will do very well. Try cooking other white fish this way, either whole small fish, fillets or steaks.

Savoury fried noodles

The possible accompaniments to noodles are almost limitless: grilled fish as in this menu, or shellfish for seafood lovers, pork, beef, chicken and duck for the carnivorous, and of course any combination of vegetables. These simple fried noodles are also an excellent basis for vegetarian meals.

Braised bamboo shoots

Preparing fresh bamboo shoots is a laborious job. It seems to take forever to peel away the outer leaves until you reach the small, tender shoots in the middle. I remember watching one of my aunts do it and being thankful it wasn't my job; apart from the tedium, these outer leaves are full of minute hairs, which hang onto your skin and can cause a most unpleasant long-lasting itch. Rubber gloves hadn't been invented in those days, or at least hadn't reached our part of Sumatra. The small shoots also need to be boiled for quite a long time before they can be sliced and used in cooking. Luckily the processing and canning of bamboo shoots overcome these problems and don't take away the crispy texture. Bamboo shoots are among the very few vegetables that are difficult to overcook. Drain the water from the can and rinse the bamboo shoots well under running water, then you can slice or dice them with a sharp knife. Sliced bamboo shoots are also available in cans, and quite recently a variety has come onto the market, already cut into pretty shapes. They are canned in Thailand and available in large oriental supermarkets. So, if you can find them in your area, use them for this recipe.

Coconut cream brûlée

The Thais and Laotians steam their coconut cream after putting it into a hollowed-out whole pumpkin. This does indeed taste very good, provided of course that you like pumpkin. The brûlée described here will be more to everybody's taste, and is less fiddly to do.

Compôte of rose-scented rhubarb

I am giving you an alternative dessert here, because not everybody likes coconut, and also because my intention is to give you, whenever I can, a seasonal ingredient that will go well with my oriental spices. Rhubarb is just at its best at this time of the year and you can still get lovely young and tender sticks; so here is a recipe I 'borrowed' from my friend Geraldene Holt, who says that this is her very favourite way of cooking and serving rhubarb.

PLANNING AND PREPARATION

You may be surprised to hear that the soufflés can be prepared in the morning – I assure you they will rise when you bake them in the evening! The coconut cream brûlé can also be prepared and cooked in the morning, and you can add the sugar in the evening just before you put them under the grill for a few minutes. The same applies to the rhubarb compôte. Everything else can be prepared quite easily in the final 60 minutes before serving.

On the day:

MORNING

Prepare the vegetables for the noodles: dice the carrots, wipe and quarter the mushrooms etc., ready for frying at the last moment.

Marinate the fish and store in the fridge; it can stay there until the evening. Prepare all the ingredients for the yellow bean sauce, i.e. make the paste and slice the onions, chillies and mushrooms.

Make the coconut cream (or prepare all the ingredients for the rhubarb compôte). Store in the fridge.

EVENING – for 8.30 dinner

6.00   Take out everything required from the fridge.
Start making the soufflé mixture ready to bake.

6.30   Fry the ingredients for the noodles, and boil the noodles for 3–4 minutes and drain. Refresh them under the cold tap, and leave to drain again.

7.00   Turn on the oven and set to 200°C/400°F/Gas Mark 6.
Cook the bamboo shoots ready to be reheated.
If you are making the halibut dish, start cooking it, and cook the mushroom mixture as well, but do not mix them yet. If you are cooking monkfish, you don't need to start grilling until the first course has been eaten.
Sprinkle the coconut cream with demerara sugar (or prepare the rhubarb in ramekins).

8.10   Put the soufflé in the oven. Heat the ingredients for the fried noodles, mix the noodles with them, and stir-fry until hot. Transfer to a heatproof serving dish, cover with aluminium foil and put in the oven.

8.30   SERVE THE SOUFFLÉ
While you are taking away the soufflé dishes, heat the bamboo shoots and either mix the halibut with the mushrooms and continue cooking until hot, or put the monkfish under the grill. Put the rhubarb compôte in the oven and don't forget to switch on the timer.

8.45   SERVE THE MAIN COURSE

For the dessert, if you are making brûlée, put it under the grill just before serving it. The compôte can be served warm or cold.

Smoked Tofu and Asparagus Soufflé

The soufflé is best if you prepare it and then bake it straight away; but you can, if need be, prepare it 4–5 hours in advance and refrigerate it until you are ready to bake it in the oven.

    250 g (8 oz) asparagus
    150 ml (¼ pint) water
    125 g (4 oz) smoked tofu
    300 ml (½ pint) milk
    50 g (2 oz) butter
    salt and pepper
    a pinch of ground coriander
    3 large eggs, separated
    25 g (1 oz) flour

Trim off the hard ends of the asparagus, and keep aside 8 of the tips, about 5 cm (2 in) long (these are to be boiled separately, for 2 minutes only, and used for decoration). Boil the rest of the asparagus in 150 ml (¼ pint) of water in a small saucepan for 4–5 minutes. Cool, then liquidize with the cooking water, and transfer into a bowl.

Using the same liquidizer, liquidize the smoked tofu until smooth. Keep aside.

Put half of the milk in a saucepan, add the butter and bring almost to boiling point. Lower the heat. Add salt, pepper and ground coriander. Beat the egg yolks and mix in the flour and the rest of the cold milk, and add this gradually to the hot milk, whipping it lightly all the time until the mixture thickens. Remove from heat and stir in the asparagus purée and smooth tofu.

Beat the egg whites until stiff and fold them into the mixture. Divide the soufflé mixture into 4 well-buttered and floured ramekins, and put two asparagus tips in each. Put the ramekins in a baking tray lined with a folded tea-towel or newspaper, and pour boiling water from a kettle into the tray so that it comes up to about the middle of the ramekins. Bake in a preheated oven at 200°C/400°F/Gas Mark 6 for 15–20 minutes. Serve immediately.

Halibut in Ginger, Garlic and Yellow Bean Sauce

The fermented yellow beans used in this recipe are common to all Far Eastern countries. The beans are available in two colours, yellow and black; both are made from soya beans.

4 halibut steaks
1 teaspoon ground white pepper
1 teaspoon granulated sugar
2 tablespoons plain flour

For the paste
2 tablespoons yellow beans
4 cloves of garlic
5-cm (2-inch) piece of fresh ginger, peeled and chopped
½ teaspoon chilli powder
1 tablespoon tamarind water or lemon juice
1 tablespoon tomato purée

Other ingredients
4 tablespoons groundnut oil
1 large onion, finely sliced
3 green chillies, seeded and finely sliced
250 g (8 oz) small button mushrooms, wiped clean and finely sliced
1 teaspoon light soy sauce
3 tablespoons *mirin* (Japanese rice wine) or dry white wine
4 tablespoons chopped spring onions

Mix the pepper, sugar and flour and spread them evenly on both sides of the fish. Leave the fish in a cool place or in the fridge while you are preparing the rest of the ingredients.

Put all the ingredients for the paste in a blender or food processor. Blend them until smooth and transfer them to a bowl.

Heat 3 tablespoons of the oil in a large non-stick frying pan. When hot add the sliced onion and green chillies. Stir-fry this mixture until it is slightly coloured, and add the fish pieces. Gently turn them over several times for about 7–8 minutes.

Remove the fish, onions and chillies onto a plate, taking care that the oil is left in the pan. Add the remaining 1 tablespoon of oil to the pan, add the mushrooms, stir-fry for 2 minutes and add the light soy sauce. Keep stirring for another minute and add the paste from the bowl. Let this simmer for 5 minutes, stirring almost all the time. Put in the fish with the onions and chillies, add the *mirin* or wine and stir again, gently so as not to break up the fish. Continue cooking on a low flame for 2 minutes. Add the chopped spring onions, cook for one minute more. Serve immediately.

Grilled Caramelised Monkfish Fillets

You will very likely be able to get, from a good fishmonger, a monkfish tail weighing about 500 g (1 lb) or a little less. Buy two of these tails, and take the flesh off the bones yourself, which is not at all difficult, and you will get 4 pieces of about equal size.

> *Other ingredients*
> 1 teaspoon salt
> 2 tablespoons lemon or lime juice
> 6 tablespoons demerara sugar

About 2 hours or less before you are ready to grill the fish, rub the pieces with the salt and lemon or lime juice and leave in a cool place. Just before it is time to grill them, coat them well with the demerara sugar. Grill for 3–4 minutes each side. Serve immediately.

Savoury Fried Noodles

Like the fried rice on page 117 this is the most basic of all the fried noodle recipes.

    250 g (8 oz) fresh or dried egg noodles
    1.25 litres (2 pints) water
    ½ teaspoon salt
    2–3 tablespoons peanut oil or sunflower oil
    4 shallots or one medium-size onion, finely sliced
    2 cloves of garlic, finely sliced
    1 teaspoon finely sliced ginger
    4 medium sized carrots, peeled and diced
    250 g (8 oz) button mushrooms, wiped clean and quartered
    2 tablespoons light soy sauce
    ¾ teaspoon ground white pepper
    ½ teaspoon sugar
    4 tablespoons hot water or chicken stock
    3 spring onions, cut into thin rounds
    salt to taste

Boil the water in a large saucepan, add the ½ teaspoon of salt, and add the noodles. If you are using fresh noodles, boil them for 1–1½ minutes; if using dried noodles, boil them for 3 minutes. Separate the noodles, using a large fork or long bamboo chopsticks, while they are boiling. Drain them in a colander and hold them under cold running water until they are cold, to stop them overcooking. Leave the noodles in the colander, turning them several times so that all the water can drain off them.

Heat the oil in a wok or large shallow saucepan (preferably a non-stick one), and fry the shallots or onion, garlic and ginger for 1 minute. Add the carrots and mushrooms, stir-fry for 2 minutes, then add the other ingredients *except* the noodles, hot water or stock, and spring onions. Keep stirring and turning the contents of the pan over for 2–3 minutes until the carrots are cooked. Add the hot water or stock, turn up the heat and add the noodles. Continue stirring, turning and tossing until the noodles are hot. Add the spring onions, and stir once more. Taste and adjust the seasoning. Transfer to a warm serving dish and serve immediately.

Braised Bamboo Shoots

Always rinse any kind of canned bamboo shoots, and if using the uncut ones, slice them into bite sizes. If you can get the bamboo shoots that have been cut into little shapes, as described on page 66, you only need to drain the can and rinse the shoots under cold running water.

    2 tablespoons peanut or sunflower oil
    625-g (1¼-lb) can of bamboo shots, drained
    2 shallots, finely sliced
    2 cloves garlic, finely sliced
    1 teaspoon finely-chopped ginger
    ½ teaspoon chilli powder
    4 tablespoons chopped spring onions or leeks
    2 tablespoons light soy sauce
    2 tablespoons *mirin* (Japanese rice wine) or dry sherry

Heat the oil in a wok or large frying pan, and stir-fry the sliced bamboo shoots for 2 minutes, then add the shallots, garlic and ginger. Stir for another minute, and add the rest of the ingredients. Stir again and simmer gently for one more minute. Adjust seasoning and serve hot with the fried noodles.

Coconut Cream Brûlée

This brûlée is best served on its own, but if you feel you need some fruit to go with it, then I recommend sliced bananas. In other seasons of course your choice will be more varied. Any summer fruits, such as strawberries, loganberries or raspberries, are excellent. In the autumn, the ideal texture to go with this coconut cream brûlée is that of figs.

    For the coconut cream
    4 eggs (size 2)
    4 tablespoons grated palm sugar or demerara sugar
    a pinch of salt
    175 ml (6 fl oz) very thick coconut milk

    To be added later
    4 teaspoons demerara sugar

Beat the eggs lightly, add the sugar, a pinch of salt and the coconut milk, and stir until the sugar is dissolved.

Divide this custard equally among 4 ramekins. Put the ramekins in a baking tray lined with a folded tea-towel or newspaper, and pour boiling water from a kettle into the tray so that it comes about halfway up the ramekins. Cook in the oven at 180°C/350°F/Gas Mark 4 for 16–18 minutes. Up to this point you can prepare everything in advance. Just before serving, sprinkle 1 teaspoon demerara sugar on top of each coconut custard, then put under the grill for about 2 minutes. Serve immediately.

Compôte of Rose-scented Rhubarb

This recipe, from Geraldene Holt's *The Gourmet Garden*, published by Pavilion (1990), is reproduced here with the author's permission.

8 leaves of rose geranium
500 g (1 lb) slim sticks of rhubarb, trimmed
90–115 g (3–4 oz) caster sugar
4 tablespoons Muscat de Beaumes de Venise
150 ml (¼ pint) single cream
1 tablespoon sugar
rose water to taste

Place a geranium leaf in four small ovenproof dishes. Cut the rhubarb diagonally into 2.5-cm (1-inch) pieces. Toss these in a bowl with the sugar and divide them among the four dishes. Put a spoonful of wine into each dish and place the remaining geranium leaves on top. Cover each dish with buttered paper.

Place the dishes on a baking sheet and cook in a preheated oven at 180°C/350°F/Gas Mark 4 for 20–25 minutes until the rhubarb is cooked. Serve the compôte hot or cold, with the cream mixed with the sugar and rose water.

Vegan Dinner for Six

I want to put at least one vegan menu into this book, as so many South-East Asian non-meat recipes are cooked without any dairy products. Coconut milk seems to be the ideal alternative.

The Menu

Sweetcorn and smoked tofu soup

◆

Wild and white rice pilaf
served with
Spiced aubergine loaf
with
Red pepper sauce
and
Tempeh and tofu cooked salad

◆

Avocado and coconut ice cream

ABOUT THE FOOD

The dishes described here make up a high-protein, high-fibre menu that uses no animal products whatever. Yet it will stand up for itself as a good meal in its own right, appealing to non-vegans for the variety of flavours and textures as well as the attractive look of the different dishes.

Sweetcorn and smoked tofu soup

Tofu is a foodstuff known for centuries in China, Japan and in all the South-East Asian countries. It has hardly any taste, but it is high in protein, contains no cholesterol, and in its countries of origin is a cheap staple for vegetarians and vegans. It is made from soya beans. For cooking, it combines well with hot and savoury ingredients or with sweet ingredients – you can make a very good ice cream with it. There are several brands of tofu now available in the West, and for this recipe smoked tofu has the best flavour. Japanese tofu is normally smoother and softer than Chinese and is particularly good for ice cream, sauces and dips; since it is pasteurised, it will keep for several months in the packet it is sold in, as long as it remains unopened. Japanese tofu is rather difficult to handle for frying, but it is quite good for this soup, if you can't get the smoked tofu.

Wild and white rice pilaf

This is a rice dish that you would not find in any traditional South-East Asian repertoire, since what is called 'wild' rice in the West does not grow in the tropics. I created the dish as a complement to the others on the menu.

Spiced aubergine loaf

You could call this an East-meets-West dish, using oriental ingredients and western cooking methods. The result is something you can carve for a non-meat main course.

Red pepper sauce

This is an alternative to the hot chilli sauce which most people in the East are accustomed to have with their meal.

Tempeh and tofu cooked salad

Tempeh (Indonesian *tempe*) is a block or cake, looking a bit like cheese but made from soya beans. The beans are cooked and then fermented with a special yeast or mould. This mould digests the part of the soya bean that human beings cannot, so the full nutritional value of the beans is preserved and indeed enhanced. Tempeh has a more interesting texture and flavour than tofu. It has become a well-known health food in North America, and is made by several small firms in Britain. Many health food shops sell tempeh, fresh or frozen; some import it from Holland.

Avocado and coconut ice cream

In Thailand, Malaysia and Indonesia you can find the most delicious coconut ice cream. It was Europeans who taught the people there how to make ice cream, but the secret of this special flavour – in Indonesia we call it *es kopyor* – lies in the kind of coconut that is used. Unfortunately these magical coconuts are not exported, but the coconut cream I use for this recipe tastes extremely good and, of course, takes the place of dairy cream in the avocado ice.

PLANNING AND PREPARATION

Make the ice cream a day or more ahead, and make the stock the day before. Prepare the aubergine loaf and the red pepper sauce on the morning of the party. If you also do all the chopping and cutting of the other ingredients several hours in advance, the last-minute cooking will take only about 30 minutes.

The day before:

Make the avocado and cococnut ice cream, and freeze.
Make the stock for the soup.

On the day:

MORNING
Prepare the aubergine loaf.
Cook the red pepper sauce.
Cut and slice all the other ingredients for all the dishes, and put them in separate containers, clingfilmed and labelled.
Keep in a cool place – some can go in the fridge.

EVENING – for 8 o'clock dinner

7.15   Start cooking the aubergine loaf.
        Cook the tofu and tempeh salad.
7.30   Make the soup.
        Cook the rice and keep it warm in the saucepan by keeping the cover tight.
8.00   SERVE THE SOUP

8.15   Transfer the ice cream from the freezer to the fridge.
       Heat the red pepper sauce.
       SERVE THE MAIN COURSES hot, warm or cold.

Sweetcorn and Smoked Tofu Soup

The sweetcorn used here is the fresh baby corn, flown in from Thailand,
that you can now get in most supermarkets and many greengrocers.

For the stock
1.5 litres (2½ pints) water
2 shallots, baked or grilled until the skins are charred
1 clove garlic, chopped
2 carrots, washed and cut into three
2 heads of baby corn, roughly chopped
2 celery stalks, cut into four
1 dried red chilli (optional)
salt to taste

The remaining ingredients
1 tablespoon groundnut or olive oil
2 shallots, finely sliced
1 teaspoon sugar
375–500 g (12–16 oz) baby corn, each head cut diagonally into three
    pieces
125 g (4 oz) smoked tofu, cut into small cubes
4 spring onions, trimmed and cut into thin rounds
2 tablespoons chopped parsley (preferably the flat-leaf kind)
1 tablespoon lemon juice
1 teaspoon light soy sauce

This stock can be made the day before and stored in the fridge until
needed. Put all the ingredients for the stock into a large saucepan.
Bring to the boil and simmer for 1 hour or a little longer. Leave the
stock to cool, then strain it into a saucepan. Discard the solids.

About half an hour before serving, heat the olive oil in a saucepan,
and fry the shallots, stirring continuously, for 1 minute. Add the sugar,
stir for another 2 minutes. Then add the sweetcorn, stir and add the
stock. Bring to the boil, simmer for 10 minutes. Add the rest of the
ingredients and continue to simmer for 3 minutes. Taste, add more salt
if necessary, and serve immediately.

Wild and White Rice Pilaf

The wild rice gives a most attractive colouring and the small amount of chilli used gives an intriguing taste.

75 g (3 oz) wild rice
225 g (8 oz) long grain white rice
(both soaked separately in cold water for 30 minutes, then drained)

The remaining ingredients
2 tablespoons groundnut or olive oil
3 shallots, finely sliced
1 clove garlic, finely chopped (optional)
600 ml (1 pint) cold water
½ teaspoon salt
a large pinch of chilli powder
2 tablespoons chopped coriander leaves (optional)
½ teaspoon ground coriander
3 tablespoons desiccated coconut
300 ml (½ pint) hot water

Heat the oil in a saucepan and fry the shallots and garlic for 1 minute, stirring continuously, then add the wild rice and stir again for another minute. Pour in the cold water and add the salt. Bring to the boil and simmer uncovered for 30 minutes. Add the white rice and the rest of the ingredients including the 300 ml (½ pint) hot water. Bring to the boil again, stir once, and cover the saucepan. Continue cooking on a low heat for 15–20 minutes or in a medium oven (150–160°C/300–325°F/Gas Mark 2–3) for up to 30 minutes. Serve hot.

Spiced Aubergine Loaf

Use a 20-cm (8-in) bread tin to mould this aubergine loaf.

3 aubergines (about 800 g/1½ lbs)
175 g (6 oz) Chinese leaves
2 shallots, finely sliced
1 teaspoon ground coriander
1 teaspoon finely-chopped ginger
a large pinch of chilli powder
1 teaspoon paprika
175 g (6 oz) can of chopped tomatoes
1 potato (about 125 g/4 oz), boiled and mashed
3 tablespoons fresh breadcrumbs
4 tablespoons chopped parsley
salt to taste
sunflower oil for frying

Wash and cut the aubergines into small cubes. Put them in a colander and sprinkle generously with salt. Leave for 30 minutes or longer. Rinse off the salt and drain them, then dry them with absorbent paper. Fry them in hot oil in two batches, and drain on absorbent paper. Blanch the Chinese leaves by plunging them for 1 minute in boiling water, then refresh them under running cold water and leave them to drain. Brush the bread tin with oil and line it with the leaves.

Heat 2 tablespoons of oil in a large frying pan and fry the shallots, stirring continuously, for 1 minute. Add the ground coriander, ginger, chilli and paprika. Stir again and add the chopped tomatoes and simmer for 10 minutes. Then add the potato, breadcrumbs and parsley. Stir this around until the potatoes and breadcrumbs have absorbed most of the liquid, then add the aubergines. Taste, and add some more salt if needed. Pack this mixture into the tin and lay some more leaves on top. Cover the tin with greaseproof paper, place it in a saucepan, pour in enough hot water to come about two-thirds of the way up the side of the tin, cover the pan and cook over a low heat for 30–40 minutes. Remove the tin from the saucepan, leave to cool, then refrigerate. Unmould the loaf before serving it cold, in thick slices. Serve with the red pepper sauce poured over it.

Red Pepper Sauce

2 shallots
1 large red pepper, seeded
4 ripe tomatoes
2 tablespoons groundnut or olive oil
½ teaspoon ground coriander
salt and pepper to taste
125 ml (4 fl oz) cold water

Chop the shallots, pepper and tomatoes coarsely. Heat the oil in a small saucepan and add the shallots and pepper. Stir for 2 minutes, then add the rest of the ingredients. Bring to the boil and simmer for 40 minutes. Taste, add more salt if necessary, then pass the mixture through a fine sieve. Refrigerate, and reheat before use.

Tempeh and Tofu Cooked Salad

425 g (14 oz) tempeh
375 g (12 oz) tofu
125 g (4 oz) beansprouts
2 green chillies, seeded and finely sliced
3 shallots, finely sliced
1 teaspoon very finely-chopped ginger
1 clove garlic, crushed
2 tablespoons mild vinegar
1 tablespoon light soy sauce
½ teaspoon mustard
1 teaspoon sugar
6 tablespoons water
salt to taste
125 ml (4 fl oz) sunflower oil for frying the tempeh and tofu

Cut the tempeh and tofu into thin pieces, about 2.5 cm (1 inch) square. Wash the beansprouts and drain in a colander.

In a non-stick frying pan fry the tempeh in several batches until it is just beginning to turn yellow. Do the same with the tofu; set these aside on absorbent paper. Discard the oil, except for 2 tablespoonsful. Fry the chillies, shallots, ginger and garlic, stirring continuously, for one minute or so; then add the vinegar, soy sauce, mustard and sugar. Stir again and add the water. Let this mixture simmer for 2 minutes, taste and add salt if needed. Now put in the fried tempeh and tofu, stir them around and add the beansprouts. Stir again and leave to simmer for just another 2 minutes. Serve warm or cold as preferred.

Avocado and Coconut Ice Cream

Long ago, when I was a child, my mother used to make a splendid avocado mousse using avocado pears from the big tree in our front garden. Her recipe was a favourite Dutch one, using condensed milk. Later in life, I decided that a combination of avocados and coconut cream would make an ideal vegan ice cream.

4 small avocado pears (weighing about 170 g/6 oz each), peeled and with
    stones removed
600 ml (1 pint) thick coconut milk (see below)
10 tablespoons icing sugar
8 tablespoons lime/lemon juice

To make the thick coconut milk you need 175 g (6 oz) desiccated coconut and 750 ml (1¼ pint) warm water. Put the desiccated coconut in a blender, add the warm water, blend for a few seconds and then strain the liquid into a bowl, squeezing the desiccated coconut a handful at a time. Discard the coconut. (There is more about coconuts and coconut milk/cream on page 27.)

Put the coconut milk into a clean blender and add the rest of the ingredients. Blend until smooth. Put the creamy mixture into an ice-cream maker or sorbetière, if you have one, and follow the manufacturer's directions. If you do not have a machine, place the mixture in a plastic container, cover and freeze. After 2 hours, when the mixture is partly frozen, remove it and beat until smooth. Repeat the process twice more during freezing, which will take about 3½–4 hours. Keep frozen until required; transfer to refrigerator 1 hour before serving.

Dinner for Eight

What I had in mind in planning this menu was a dinner party that could be entirely prepared and cooked at least a day in advance. Then, on the day itself, you can join your guests on a sightseeing tour, or whatever, instead of having to stay at home just to make the dinner. Or you can all go to the theatre without worrying about what you will eat afterwards.

The Menu

Chicken and galingale soup with sweet basil

◆

Javanese lamb curry
served with
Plain cooked rice
and
Spiced braised okra

◆

Pineapple parfait

ABOUT THE FOOD

Chicken and galingale soup with sweet basil

In South-East Asia soup is normally eaten throughout the meal. In most restaurants in South-East Asia you get a 'steamboat' placed in the middle of your table which keeps the soup piping hot for everyone to help themselves throughout the meal. But for a dinner party at home, it is more practical to serve this soup as a first course. This particular soup is what the people of Thailand called *Kai Tom Ka*. The best *Kai Tom Ka* I ever had was served in a steamboat in a famous food bazaar called

Silom Village in the centre of Bangkok. We ate it as a first course while we waited for our fish, chosen from a glass-walled aquarium, while, not far from our table, lobsters from large baskets full to the brim were grilling merrily on a long charcoal brazier.

Javanese lamb curry

In almost every town in Central Java, you will find street food vendors selling this freshly-cooked curry, which we call *Gulé Kambing*. Their customers are office workers or students or local residents, who bring their own containers from home and take the *gulé* back to be eaten with plain cooked rice, either for lunch or as an early supper around 6 in the evening or a later supper at around 10 o'clock. The curry will be both chilli-hot and piping hot; the vendor, who is usually a man, puts the huge pot to bubble constantly over a large charcoal brazier. The meat used in Java is always goat meat. Here I suggest you use lamb, from the leg or shoulder. This is one of the many oriental dishes that will actually improve by being kept for up to 24 hours or so after cooking.

Plain cooked rice

Even though my recipe here is not chilli-hot, it is still quite spicy, so the best thing to eat with it is plain cooked rice that will absorb the spiciness of the curry.

Spiced braised okra

South-East Asian countries have, in my experience, two basic ways of eating fresh vegetables. The first is to eat them raw or very lightly cooked, without spices but with hot relishes or peanut sauce. The other way is to cook or stir-fry the vegetables with spices. Okra is a particularly good vegetable to accompany this lamb curry. But if you can't get or don't like okra, substitute for it French beans, which can be cooked in exactly the same way.

Pineapple parfait

This is the easiest way to preserve fruit for a day or so in the freezer. The result is a very simple but exquisite dessert, especially good after a spicy meal.

PLANNING AND PREPARATION

Everything will be ready in a surprisingly short time if you just concentrate on preparing and cooking all in one go – maybe as soon as you come back from shopping. If you have a microwave oven, the rice also can be cooked in advance, ready to be reheated in the microwave on full power for 4 minutes. If you have an electric rice cooker, then ideally you should cook the rice in the 20 minutes that it takes to heat up the rest of the meal. Even cooking rice in the old-fashioned way, using a single saucepan, only takes 20 minutes. (See the section on 'Cooking rice', page 25.)

The day before:

Make the parfait and freeze it.
Prepare and cook everything else except the rice.
Store these in the fridge.

On the day:

EVENING – for 9 o'clock dinner
8.35   Take everything out of the fridge.
8.40   Cook the rice.
        Heat the soup and the lamb curry.
9.00   SERVE THE SOUP
9.15   Heat the okra while putting everything else into serving dishes.
9.20   Transfer the parfait from the freezer to the fridge.
        SERVE THE MAIN COURSE

Chicken and Galingale Soup with Sweet Basil

This soup must not be bland! Use fresh lemon grass, galingale and coriander leaves if you possibly can, and coconut milk made from freshly-grated or desiccated coconut. This is quick and easy if you have a food processor or blender, or even if you do it entirely by hand; full instructions are given on page 28. Canned or powdered coconut milk can be used, but gives a less satisfactory result.

For the stock
4 large chicken breasts, on the bone
1.5 litres (2½ pints) cold water
4 stems of lemon grass, washed and bruised
10-cm (4-inch) piece of galingale, peeled and sliced
4 kaffir lime leaves
4 shallots, sliced
3 small dried red chillies

To finish the soup
250 g (8 oz) fresh shiitake mushrooms, stalks removed and added to the
    stock pot, the mushrooms sliced thinly
4 cooked chicken breasts, sliced (i.e. the ones that were in the stock)
2 tablespoons lime or lemon juice
1 tablespoon fish sauce
a large pinch of chilli powder
salt to taste
250 ml (8 fl oz) very thick coconut milk (page 28)
3 tablespoons chopped basil leaves

Put all the ingredients for the stock, including the mushroom stalks, in a saucepan, boil them for 15 minutes, then take out the chicken breasts. Bone and skin the breasts, slice them thinly and keep them aside. Put the bones and the skin back into the stockpot and continue cooking the stock for 30 more minutes.

Strain the stock through a fine sieve into another saucepan. You should have just a little more than 900 ml (1½ pints) of this stock. Bring it back to the boil, and add the mushrooms and the rest of the ingredients (except the coconut milk and basil leaves). Simmer the mixture for 3 minutes, adjust the seasoning, and add the coconut milk. Simmer gently for 3 more minutes, stirring most of the time to prevent the coconut milk from boiling. Just before serving, put the basil leaves into the very hot soup, to cook them just a little. Serve hot, with the chicken breasts and mushrooms divided equally among the soup bowls.

Javanese Lamb Curry

The best way to cook this curry, if you don't want the meat to be cooked too long (as it often is, in the traditional Javanese way), is to cook and reduce the sauce first, then put in the lamb towards the end, for about

10–20 minutes only. Trim off and throw away all the fat except about 50 g (2 oz), where it is thickest, and cook the bones and the less good parts of the meat along with the sauce. These unwanted solids will be disposed of when you strain the sauce through a coarse strainer after cooking.

1.5 kg (3½ lb) lamb, leg or shoulder, cut into 4-cm (1½-inch) pieces
600 ml (1 pint) hot water
900 ml (1½ pints) coconut milk made from 175 g (6 oz) desiccated
    coconut

For the paste
4 shallots or 1 onion, chopped
2 cloves of garlic, chopped
1 tablespoon chopped fresh ginger
5 candlenuts (page 11) or 8 blanched almonds
2 teaspoons ground coriander
1 teaspoon ground cinnamon
1 teaspoon chilli powder
¼ teaspoon galingale powder
½ teaspoon turmeric powder
2 cloves
¼ teaspoon ground white pepper
6 tablespoons coconut milk
1 teaspoon salt

To be added later
5-cm (2-inch) piece of lemon grass, washed
2 kaffir lime leaves or 1 bay leaf
3 tamarind slices
½ teaspoon brown sugar
more salt to taste

Put all the ingredients for the paste in a blender or food processor, and blend until smooth. Transfer this paste into a large saucepan, heat and bring it to the boil, then stir continuously for 4–5 minutes. Add the bones, fat and meat trimmings, stir and add the hot water. Cover the saucepan, and simmer for 20 minutes.

Remove the saucepan lid and skim off the brown froth, then add the coconut milk, bring the contents back to the boil and simmer for 45 minutes, stirring often. Strain the contents of the pan through a coarse sieve into another saucepan. Discard bones and all the other solids. Put the saucepan with the sauce back on the stove, add the remaining ingredients. Bring it to the boil and simmer for 15–20 minutes to reduce the sauce further; it will now be quite thick, but remember it is not finished yet. Bring the sauce to a rolling boil, and add the lamb pieces. Cook on a high heat, stirring often, for 10–20 minutes, depending on how well-done you like the meat to be. Cool and refrigerate until needed.

Reheat the curry in a saucepan, stirring continuously when the sauce comes to the boil, for 3 minutes. Adjust the seasoning, remove the lemon grass, kaffir lime leaves and tamarind slices, and serve immediately.

Plain Cooked Rice

Maybe the quantity of rice specified here is a little too much; it is quite difficult for me, as an oriental born in a rice-eating society, to judge how much rice a European will eat at a dinner party. But with spicy curry anyone will need quite a generous helping of rice.

875 g (1½ lb) Thai fragrant, Basmati or Patna rice
900 ml (1½ pints) cold water

Wash the rice in a bowl with two changes of water, and drain well. Then transfer the rice into a thick-bottomed saucepan. Add the water and bring to the boil. Simmer the rice, uncovered, for about 10 minutes, until all the water has been absorbed. Stir the rice once, then put on the cover very tightly. Lower the heat and leave the rice to finish cooking for another 10 minutes. The rice is now ready to serve.

Alternatively, after the first 10 minutes, the rice can be transferred into a steamer and then steamed for 10 minutes. Or you can transfer the rice into a bowl, cover it loosely with clingfilm or with a plate, and microwave it on full power for 5 minutes.

Spiced Braised Okra

Okra or ladies' fingers have a rather oily texture, which may be what has prevented them becoming really popular in the West; but when people have eaten them once or twice they usually like them. They are not difficult to get, at least in large towns, because they are so important to Indian cooking. Choose young ones, which are smaller in size. To prepare them simply trim off a little bit of the bottom part, which is rather hard.

    3 tablespoons vegetable oil
    4 shallots, finely sliced
    3 cloves of garlic, finely sliced
    3 large green chillies, seeded and sliced into thin rounds
    1 teaspoon ground coriander
    ½ teaspoon ground cumin
    3 ripe tomatoes, skinned and seeded, then roughly chopped
    750 g (1½ lb) young okra, washed, then trimmed and patted dry
    ½ teaspoon sugar
    ½ teaspoon salt
    2 tablespoons chopped coriander leaves or flat-leaf parsley

Heat the oil in a wok or frying pan, and fry the shallots, garlic and green chillies, stirring them continuously, for 2 minutes. Add the ground coriander and cumin, stir again and add the chopped tomatoes and okra. Stir, then cover the wok or pan and simmer for 4 minutes. Remove the cover, and add the sugar and salt. Stir the okra again for one minute. Adjust the seasoning, and add the coriander leaves or parsley. Stir for 30 seconds.

If the okra are not to be served straight away, leave them to cool in the wok or pan. When cold, cover it and keep in a cool place. Reheat in the wok or pan, stirring them often, for 2–3 minutes, or until hot.

Pineapple Parfait

Serve the parfait like ice cream, accompanied by almond biscuits if you wish.

   1 medium-size ripe pineapple
   600 ml (1 pint) double cream
   4 egg whites
   a pinch of salt
   200 g (7 oz) caster sugar

With a sharp knife cut away the plume and base of the pineapple. Then remove the skin in strips, quite thickly so that the eyes are removed at the same time. Wash the whole pineapple under running cold water. Then cut it in half lengthways, and carefully remove the core. Cut each half into 8–10 thin long wedges, then chop these into tiny pieces. Keep the chopped pineapple with the juice in a large glass bowl.

With a hand-held electric beater, whisk the cream until thick but not too stiff, and keep it aside. Put the egg white in another bowl, add the pinch of salt and whisk it until stiff. Then add half the sugar, while you continue whisking until the mixture stands in peaks. Add the remaining sugar, whisk the egg whites for 30 seconds more. Using a metal spoon, fold in the cream and add the chopped pineapple a little at a time, stirring gently. Transfer the parfait into a plastic container, cover and freeze until required.

Take the parfait out of the freezer 20 minutes before serving.

Summer

Once in a while, I enjoy cooking for a big party, especially if all I have to do is cook – someone else sends the invitations, folds the napkins into funny shapes, polishes the glasses and cleans up afterwards. The largest number I ever cooked for was 200, which is not considered a big crowd in Indonesia, where neighbours, friends and relations can be counted on to help. This party, however, wasn't in Indonesia. I was catering for an organisation. Apart from two or three very close friends, I couldn't expect my neighbours to help, since they were not coming to the party. The only relations within reach were a husband and two young sons. It was summer, late summer just turning towards autumn. This was fortunate, not because the party could be held out of doors – it was a rather grand affair that took place somewhere in the City – but because it gave us a chance to thaw the fish. The fish was an opah.

I met my first opah – *Lampris cuttatus* or *L. regius* – at a dinner at the house of Alan Davidson, the author of several famous books on fish and how to cook them. Jane Grigson described, in *Fish Cookery*, an opah that she and her husband, Geoffrey Grigson, saw to their astonishment in a fish shop in Swindon in 1971: 'a taut oval up to six feet long . . . softly spotted with white. The main blue-grey and green of its skin reflects an iridescence of rose, purple and gold. The fins are a brilliant red.' These creatures, in English called sometimes sunfish and sometimes moonfish, are rare in northern waters, though they do feature in Alan Davidson's *North Atlantic Seafood*.

Through a fishmonger Alan knew at Billingsgate, I learned that an opah had turned up in the nets of a Dutch trawler a month or two earlier and was now reposing in the Billingsgate cold store. A price was agreed, and about ten days before the dinner we took the car to Billingsgate to collect the fish. This was the old Billingsgate market, which some experts predicted would fall down when the fish market moved to its new building in Docklands and the ice in the cold store, which was more than a century old, was allowed to melt. This has not happened, but the ice-cave was certainly impressive. The opah, which was over four feet long and weighed nearly fifty kilos, was found and loaded into the boot of the car. Back home, we had to get it out again and onto the carefully-scrubbed operating table in the back of the garage. This was when we had to turn to our neighbour and ask for help. It took a little while to persuade him that this was a serious request. But we were only working on the Indonesian principle of *gotong-royong* – that is, when *he* needed to lift a large fish from his car, we would of course help *him*.

The fish took many days to thaw, and we obviously could not leave it uncut until it thawed through; the outer layers would have started to go off. So twice a day we carved out huge steaks and opah fillets to be marinated and cooked ready for the party. The 200 guests accounted for only half of the opah, for there were a great many other dishes; the rest I made into pâté for my husband to put into sandwiches for his lunch at the Poly. He said that Poly friends were still making occasional opah pâté jokes five years later.

Strange things sometimes happened at the Poly. My husband once taught on a short course in English for Scandinavian accountants; at the final meeting, when all the staff were gathered in the classroom to say goodbye, two of the participants came in with their present for the teachers – half a pig, fresh from Smithfield and cleft neatly from nose to tail. One of the lecturers, who had taught in Norway for some years, whispered to my husband: 'This is a Scandinavian joke. They want to see how we react.' The lecturers thanked the accountants, said they trusted the other half of the pig would be produced after next year's course, and carried the carcase into the kitchen of a nearby restaurant, where it was professionally butchered. A shop was raided for a supply of plastic bags and every lecturer returned home with enough pork to last many days. The only problem was the head. I met my husband at Waterloo station to catch the train home. He showed me the plastic bags he was carrying, and said: 'Everyone decided you should have the head, because you would know how to cook it.' I had hardly ever cooked pork before, let alone the head. But without too much thinking I put the pig's head into a casserole, drowned it with a bottle of red wine and seasoned it well with chillies, onions and plenty of garlic and ginger. Then I cooked it in a slow oven for many hours, really cooked it to death. The result was extremely good.

I suppose we all have our favourite number for a party, rather depending on how many we can comfortably seat. I have never yet managed to own a dining-room big enough and square enough for a round table, but I will – one day, somehow. Indonesians love round tables with a lazy-Susan turntable in the middle – you see them in some upmarket Chinese restaurants – because, like the Chinese, we have many dishes on the table together and people need to be able to help themselves frequently. Tables like this generally seat ten or twelve, and you can talk to the person opposite you almost as easily as to your neighbour, which is very civilised. Much as I love my food, I cannot imagine a dinner without conversation. In my first year at university, I started to read English Literature and felt immediately at home in the novels of Jane Austen, not because I had much experience of the life of a country landowner but because in her characters' conversation I recognised the tones of polite Javanese society: measured, conventional, but edged with wit and sharpened by the enjoyment of language. I have heard or read somewhere that the best dinner parties are inspired by malice, and though I have never maliciously invited known enemies to sit down together, I do like to see a little bit of competition and some differences of opinion. Ten or twelve people around a table that has no obvious 'head' are ideal for this. I possess a square Victorian schoolroom table (it must have come from a schoolroom because it is stained with ink, and I daresay with children's tears, which leave no mark), and this seats two on a side, so for the time being I find eight a very convivial number.

I admit there are no pig's heads in my summer menus, though there is some pork; there is no opah, though you could put some in the seafood salad. (If you do, try to find a younger, smaller one than mine. Fifty kilos means a rather tough old fish. Go for a 25-kilo opah, like the one Alan Davidson describes in his book.) I have been led astray to discuss these things by considering the pleasures of cooking for a large party, one of which is that – if you're lucky – the preparations become a social occasion in themselves. The two best times of the year for entertaining everyone together must surely be midwinter and midsummer, the opposite sides of the round table of the year – another table at which there is no obvious head.

Dinner for Four

My first menu here is an intimate dinner for four, and almost everything can be prepared in advance. Only the rice and the green beans, and the final stage of cooking the meat, need to be done at the last moment. You may find it a good idea to make some omelette webs just for yourself one day, by way of getting some practice. They are not at all difficult, but a little experience is always a help.

The Menu

Mushrooms stuffed with crabmeat and chicken, wrapped in omelette webs

◆

Beef in sesame seeds with chilli and garlic
served with
Steamed Thai fragrant rice
and
Spiced baked aubergine with spiced green beans

◆

Creamed mango layer cake

ABOUT THE FOOD

Mushrooms stuffed with crabmeat and chicken

In the East we often stuff vegetables and fish, not only because they taste good, but because they can take a lot of time to make; taking time and trouble is one way we like to show respect for our guests. These stuffed mushrooms in fact won't take a lot of your time, unless of course you want to start with a live crab, boil it and crack the shell and pick out the meat yourself. That may be perfection, but for this dish I do not disapprove of canned crabmeat. The kind that is canned in Thailand, with just the white meat, is very good indeed. These cans are widely available in large supermarkets. The recipe for the stuffing is also Thai, although it was originally intended for tomatoes stuffed with pork. I use chicken instead of pork here.

Beef in sesame seeds

This is my version of the famous Korean beef dish called *bulgogi*. As with so many other meat dishes from the East, the secret lies in the marinade. I ate a most delicious *bulgogi* in the smartest and most expensive Korean restaurant in Jakarta in 1987, and since then I have been experimenting with the ingredients in different proportions. Linda Sue Park, the winner of the first Taittinger cookery competition run in conjunction with *The Independent* newspaper, gave me her recipe for *bulgogi*, which is very good, though here I suggest a larger quantity of the sesame seeds and the hot spices. Linda Sue also proposed that the *bulgogi* should be eaten with *kimchee* (Korean pickled cabbage); they certainly go well together, but I suggest this as the first course for another menu (which you may like to plan yourself), or for lunch. The recipe for *kimchee* is on page 199.

Traditional Korean *bulgogi* is grilled and served without a sauce. The sauce here is my own addition, because my family prefer their food with sauce, especially if it is to be eaten with rice. The beef is fried rather than grilled, mainly because it is simpler to put thin slices into a wok or a frying pan than to arrange them on a grill, but also because fried leftovers are better for reheating. But you can grill the beef, and leave out the sauce, if you prefer – it will then be a more authentic *bulgogi*.

Thai fragrant rice

I have put the name of the rice into the menu because 'Thai fragrant' sounds much more attractive than just plain boiled or steamed rice. More information about this rice, and instructions for steaming it, will be found on pages 18 and 25–26.

Spiced baked aubergine and spiced green beans

The spice mix described here is a basic combination that I use a lot in my cooking. It goes equally well with other vegetables. If you don't want to make the spice mixture, you can mix the sliced baked aubergine with the beans and then, while still hot, toss them with your own favourite vinaigrette and serve them warm or cold.

Creamed mango layer cake

This is a recipe which I have developed from what in Java we call *Kue lapis agar-agar*. A cake of different-coloured layers, made from ordinary rice flour and glutinous rice flour, or from tapioca or cornflour, is a popular sweet sold by street food vendors all over Java. The layers made with agar-agar (a seaweed gelatine, which has no taste whatsoever) are usually flavoured with different fruit purées or juices. To make creamy ones we use coconut cream. Agar-agar is a good gelatine to use in the tropics, because it will gel without refrigeration, and the cake will stay firm while it is waiting to be served and eaten. However, it has a more rubbery texture than gelatine made from pig's trotters, if you use just a little too much of it.

This creamed mango cake is not made with agar-agar, but with ordinary gelatine, which is of course available everywhere. I also use whipped cream and egg yolks to make the mango mousse layer of the cake, a process that may be more familiar to most people in the West than making and using coconut cream.

The quantities given here are sufficient for 8 people; the cake is so good that I am sure you will have no problem finishing the leftovers yourself. Also, by doubling the ingredients of the other dishes, you can easily convert this whole menu to provide dinner for 8 people. If you do this, you may find it a bonus not to have to double the quantities for making this creamy cake.

PLANNING AND PREPARATION

I suggest you do the shopping the day before the dinner, and marinate the beef in the fridge overnight. You can also make the mango cake the day before, or early on the morning of the party.

On the day of the dinner, whenever you have a more or less

uninterrupted hour in the kitchen, stuff the mushrooms and prepare the aubergines, so that they will be ready to go into the oven 25 minutes before you sit down for the first course. During this hour you can also top and tail the green beans and blanch them, prepare the spice mixture, and make the omelette webs. Put the rice to boil and simmer before you join your guests for the first course. Directions for cooking rice are on page 25.

The day before:

Make the mango cake and refrigerate until required.
Marinate the beef.

On the day:

MORNING

Prepare the mushrooms and stuff them.
Make the omelette webs and store them in the fridge.
Prepare the ingredients for the sauce; keep in the fridge.
Prepare the spice mix for aubergine and beans.
Blanch the beans.
Put the aubergine in a heatproof dish with the spice mix, ready to put in the oven in the evening.

EVENING – for 8.30 dinner

8.00   Turn on the oven to 180°C/350°F/Gas Mark 4.
        Take everything out of the fridge, except the mango cake.

8.10   Put the mushrooms and aubergine in the oven to cook.
        Start cooking the rice.
        Fry the beef and keep warm.

8.25   Heat the beans and mix in the prepared spice mix.

8.30   Wrap mushrooms in omelette webs and serve.

8.45   Heat the sauce for the beef, add the beef and stir-fry for 2
        minutes until hot. Serve immediately with aubergine and beans
        and rice.

Mushrooms Stuffed with Crabmeat and Chicken, Wrapped in Omelette Webs

Allow four mushrooms per person, and serve them on a bed of salad leaves dressed with vinaigrette. Choose the ordinary standard-size cultivated mushrooms that open into a cup just right for stuffing.

16 standard-size mushrooms, wiped or peeled and the stalks removed
3 tablespoons olive oil

For the stuffing
125 g (4 oz) chicken breast, without skin
125 g (4 oz) crabmeat, white meat only
3 cloves garlic, finely chopped
1 large or 2 small red chillies, seeded and finely chopped
2 kaffir lime leaves, finely shredded
1 cm (½ inch) fresh ginger, peeled and finely chopped
2 tablespoons finely-chopped coriander leaves or parsley
3 spring onions, outer leaves discarded, cut into thin rounds
1 tablespoon fish sauce or 1 teaspoon salt
1 egg yolk

For the omelette webs
3 eggs (size 2) + 1 egg white
vegetable oil

Chop the chicken meat, put it in a food processor and process until smooth. Put it in a glass bowl, and add all the ingredients for the stuffing. Using a wooden spoon, mix the stuffing well. Chill for 10–15 minutes.

Put the oil in another bowl, add the mushrooms, and with your hand mix them well until the mushrooms are well coated with the oil.

Oil an ovenproof dish large enough to take all 16 mushrooms side by side in a single layer. Stuff the mushrooms and arrange them on the dish. Cover the dish with clingfilm and refrigerate until ready to cook. Remove the clingfilm before putting the dish in the preheated oven at 180°C/350°F/Gas Mark 4 for 25 minutes.

To make the webs
Break the eggs into a bowl, add the extra egg white, and with a fork break the yolks. Do not beat, but just gently mix the yolks and the

whites with the fork. Oil a round non-stick frying pan; when the pan is hot, start making the omelette webs. Pour some of the egg mix into a small wire sieve, and very quickly make a pattern of a spider's web or a net with the egg dribbling through the sieve. Transfer the cooked omelette web to a flat plate, and continue making more webs until you have used up all the egg. Keep in a cool place until ready to use.

Use the omelette webs to wrap the hot stuffed mushrooms loosely. Arrange the mushrooms on top of the salad. Serve warm or cold.

Beef in Sesame Seeds with Chilli and Garlic

Whether you make this by frying or grilling, with or without sauce (page 94), the meat should be marinated overnight.

750 g (1½ lb) rump steak or sirloin steak, sliced as thinly as possible across the grain
8 tablespoons vegetable oil for frying

For the marinade
2 tablespoons white sesame seeds
2 shallots, peeled and chopped
3 cloves garlic, peeled and chopped
2 small dried red chillies
2.5 cm (1 inch) fresh ginger, peeled
½ teaspoon sugar
¼ teaspoon salt
1 tablespoon light soy sauce
2 tablespoons groundnut or olive oil

For the sauce
1 tablespoon tomato purée
1½ tablespoons *mirin* (Japanese rice wine) or dry sherry
1½ tablespoons light soy sauce
a large pinch of chilli powder

Put all the ingredients for the marinade in a blender, and blend until smooth. Transfer this paste into a glass bowl, add the slices of beef and mix well. Cover the bowl with clingfilm and refrigerate overnight.

Heat the vegetable oil in a wok or a large frying pan, and fry the beef in two batches for only 2 minutes each time. Drain the fried beef in a colander. (This can be done in advance.)

Just a few minutes before serving, mix the ingredients for the sauce in the wok or frying pan, heat for one minute and add the meat. Stir the meat around until hot – but not longer than 2 minutes. Serve immediately with the rice and vegetables.

Spiced Baked Aubergine with Spiced Green Beans

2 large aubergines, washed, then wiped dry with a paper towel
500 g (1 lb) French or Kenya beans, topped and tailed

For the spice mix
3 tablespoons olive oil
2 large onions, peeled and chopped
4 cloves garlic, peeled and chopped
1 large green chilli, seeded and finely chopped, or ½ teaspoon chilli
   powder
1 teaspoon ground coriander
¼ teaspoon grated nutmeg
1 tablespoon tomato purée
1 tablespoon fish sauce
½ teaspoon sugar (optional)
4 tablespoons chopped parsley (preferably the flat-leaf kind)
1 tablespoon chopped coriander leaf (optional)
¼ teaspoon salt

To pre-cook the spice mix, heat the oil in a wok or a saucepan and fry the onions and garlic, stirring all the time, for 3 minutes. Then add the rest of the ingredients, except the parsley and coriander leaves and the salt. Stir and simmer for 2 minutes. Add the remaining ingredients, stir again and turn off the heat. Taste and add more salt if necessary. Set the mixture aside, in its wok or saucepan, until needed.

You can bake the aubergines whole while you are preparing the other things in this menu. Put them on a rack in a preheated oven at 200°C/400°F/Gas Mark 6 for 35 minutes. Cool, then peel them and cut into thick slices. Arrange the slices on an oiled ovenproof dish. Season with some salt and freshly-ground black pepper. Spread half of the spice mix on top of the aubergines; keep in a cool place until ready to bake them again, uncovered, in the oven at the same temperature as before, for 20–25 minutes.

Blanch the beans in boiling water for 2 minutes. Drain and put them straight into a bowl of very cold water. Leave them there for 2 minutes, then drain and keep them aside until just before you serve the main course. Heat up the remaining spice mix, add the beans, mix thoroughly and heat through for about 3 minutes.

Creamed Mango Layer Cake

First of all you need a square glass or ceramic pie dish, about 18 × 18 cm (7½ × 7½ inches) or a round one 20 cm (8 inches) in diameter. It should be at least 7.5 cm (3 inches) deep. The cake will be easy to slice, and you will not have the hassle of turning it out from a mould. You will also need a hand-held electric beater.

The cake consists of three layers: mango slices top and bottom, with a layer of mango mousse in between.

You need three large ripe mangoes. Peel them, and slice them into julienne strips. Reserve half the total – the best-looking slices, weighing about 750 g (1½ lb) – for the bottom and top layers of the cake. Put the rest into a blender or food processor and blend until smooth. Transfer to a large glass bowl.

Start with the mango slices for the bottom layer.

For one layer of mango slices (you will need the same ingredients again for the
top layer, which you should prepare after making the mousse)
15 g (½ oz) powdered gelatine
1 tablespoon lemon juice
250 ml (8 fl oz) freshly-squeezed orange juice
4 tablespoons granulated sugar
375 g (12 oz) mango slices

Put the gelatine in a small saucepan, add 3 tablespoons of cold water and leave for about 5 minutes until the water has been absorbed.

Strain the lemon and orange juice into another saucepan, add the sugar, and bring them to the boil. Stir to dissolve the sugar. Let this liquid boil vigorously for 5–6 minutes. Heat the softened gelatine until melted, and pour it into the orange and lemon juice mixture. Take the pan off the heat, let it cool a little and stir in the mango slices. Pour them into the dish and refrigerate. While waiting for it to set, proceed with making the mango mousse as follows.

For the mango mousse
15 g (½ oz) powdered gelatine
4 eggs (size 2)
5 tablespoons caster sugar
250 ml (8 fl oz) double cream

Put the gelatine into a small saucepan, add 3 tablespoons of cold water, and leave it until the water has been absorbed or until you are ready to melt the gelatine and mix it with the mousse.

Put the eggs in a heatproof bowl, and put this on top of a saucepan half filled with simmering water. Using a hand-held electric beater, whisk the eggs at high speed for 2 minutes. Add the sugar while still beating, and continue beating for another 5 minutes or until the eggs become very light and thick. Take the bowl from the heat and whisk until the contents are cool. When cool, pour this into the mango purée, and mix them well together. Heat the saucepan with the gelatine and stir until the gelatine is completely melted. Take the pan off the heat and continue stirring for a minute or so, then pour the liquid gelatine into the mango and egg mousse. Fold the gelatine and mousse gently together. In another bowl, whip the cream until it has the same consistency as the mousse, and fold this into the mousse.

By now the mango slices in the fridge will have set. Take them out of the fridge, and carefully pour the mousse on top. Level the mousse with the back of a spoon and put it back in the fridge for 15 minutes. In the meantime prepare the top layer of mango slices in the same way as the bottom one. When they are cool, and after the mousse has been in the fridge for at least 15 minutes so that it has become quite firm, gently spread the mango slices and the juice on top of the mousse. Refrigerate for at least 4 hours or overnight.

To serve the cake, cut it with a large knife that has been wetted with hot water, and lift each slice out of the dish with a cake slice or spatula.

Dinner for Six

This is a lovely meal for a summer evening, or a hot summer day; the salmon and mango salad is as cool as a fish under a stone. The remarkable thing is that it seems to go equally well on a cold winter's night. The main course is sustaining but not heavy. As for the pavlova, we can only marvel that something so simple should be so classically, lusciously self-indulgent.

The Menu

Thai mango salad with salmon

◆

Medallions of pork with mushrooms in green peppercorn sauce
served with
Singapore rice noodles
and
Yard-long beans in coconut dressing

◆

Pavlova with strawberries

ABOUT THE FOOD

Thai mango salad with salmon

The mango salad that I had on my first visit to Bangkok some years ago was made with green unripe mango, lightly cooked and mixed with spiced minced pork. The combination of flavours was very good, but I realised even then that a combination of ripe mango and fish would be more acceptable to European and American palates. When I made this for my dinner guests back in London, it became popular straight away and has been much in demand ever since. The recipe has appeared in

Taste magazine in one of its '30-minute menu' columns. In this version, however, I have included the aromatic herbs that always play a part in any Thai salad.

Medallions of pork with mushrooms in green peppercorn sauce

Quite a long name for a very simple dish; I have made a lot of improvements on the original recipe that I learned from a Chinese friend long ago in my student days in Central Java. You will find this dish, which is basically just pork on soy sauce, in Singaporean, Vietnamese and Malaysian restaurants. I am sure the Filipinos, Laotians and Burmese have very similar dishes, differing in small details only. I have made my version look more like a homecooked dinner-party dish than something you would get in a restaurant.

Singapore rice noodles

This, too, is something that everyone who has been to Singapore has enjoyed in restaurants and cafés, where the noodles are usually mixed with large prawns, crabmeat, squid and many other sea creatures. The effect is very easy to reproduce at home, and you can indulge your fancy with as many different kinds of seafood as are available at the fishmonger's.

Yard-long beans in coconut dressing

If you think the coconut dressing is going to take too much of your time to make, then at any rate try the yard-long beans. Choose them carefully: fresh ones snap easily and are nice and crisp. Tired ones are stringy. They can be eaten raw, or you can boil them in slightly-salted water for 4–6 minutes until they are tender.

Pavlova with strawberries

I can't resist strawberries for a summer dinner party – why indeed should anyone want to resist? Serving them with, or on top of, a pavlova is the ideal way. I assure you the recipe I give here will work every time. I have made dozens of pavlovas like this, and only once had a flop; that was because I had just got a new oven with a temperature control in degrees Celsius instead of Fahrenheit, and I miscalculated the conversion.

PLANNING AND PREPARATION

The best time to prepare this menu is the morning of the party. Everything will turn out just right and look very fresh, and there will be no last-minute cooking at all. The only thing that you will need to do is to spread the whipped cream on the meringue just before you serve the pavlova; the strawberries are in a separate bowl so that your guests can help themselves.

On the day:

MORNING

Make pavlova, when ready keep covered in a cool place.

Clean the strawberries and refrigerate.

Cook the salmon. Leave to cool at room temperature, then chill until required.

Prepare mango and salad leaves and refrigerate.

Fry the mushrooms and the medallions of pork.

Prepare the rest of the ingredients.

Cut up and slice all ingredients for the noodles.

Blanch the beans and prepare the coconut dressing. Put all these in the fridge.

EVENING – for 8.30 dinner

6.00　　Take everything out of the fridge.

Cook the noodles and keep in a heatproof dish covered with aluminium foil.

8.00　　Turn on oven to 180°C/350°F/Gas Mark 4.

Put the noodles in the oven to heat.

Boil water to finish cooking the beans.

Beat the cream for the pavlova and keep in the fridge.

8.15　　Finish cooking the pork.

Finish cooking the beans and roll them in the coconut dressing.

Turn the oven down to 130°C/250°F/Gas Mark ½.

Put everything that needs to be warmed in the oven.

Spread the cream on the pavlova and keep in a cool place (or this can be done after you finish the main course).

8.30　　SERVE THE MANGO AND SALMON SALAD

8.45　　SERVE THE MAIN COURSES

Thai Mango Salad with Salmon

Buy salmon fillets that are already cut to the right size for this salad, as this saves a lot of time. Choose mangoes that still feel slightly hard.

For the mango salad
2 medium-size mangoes, peeled and cut into julienne strips
½ teaspoon salt
1 tablespoon lime or lemon juice
some mixed varieties of lettuce leaves
12–14 coriander or mint leaves

For the fish
2 tablespoons peanut or olive oil
1 onion, finely sliced
2 cloves garlic, crushed
1 large red chilli, seeded and finely chopped
5-cm (2-inch) piece of lemon grass, outer leaves discarded, finely chopped
5-cm (2-inch) piece of fresh ginger, peeled and finely chopped
2–3 kaffir lime leaves, finely shredded (optional)
2 tablespoons fish sauce (*nam pla*) or light soy sauce
2 tablespoons white wine vinegar
125 ml (4 fl oz) hot water
6 salmon fillets, about 100–125 g (3½–4 oz) each

Put the mango slices in a bowl, and sprinkle with salt and lime or lemon juice.

Use the mixed lettuce and coriander or mint leaves to line a serving dish.

Heat the oil in a large frying pan and fry all the chopped and sliced ingredients, stirring all the time, for 2 minutes. Add the fish sauce and vinegar and water, and simmer for another 2 minutes. Then add the fish. Let everything simmer for 3–4 minutes, turning over the fish pieces once. Remove from the heat and leave to cool.

When the fish is cool, arrange the mango strips on top of the lettuce leaves and the fish on top of the mangoes, then pour the cooking juices over the salad. Chill, but take out of the fridge about 10 minutes before serving.

Medallions of Pork with Mushrooms
in Green Peppercorn Sauce

You can cut attractive medallions if you get tenderloin of pork. Allow 4–5 medallions per person. If you can't get the fresh green peppercorns, which are now widely available in ethnic shops and in some large supermarkets, use freshly-ground black pepper.

1 kg (2 lb) tenderloin of pork, cut into medallions
500 g (1 lb) button mushrooms, cut into quarters or halves
150 ml (¾ pint) groundnut oil for frying

For the marinade
1 tablespoon light soy sauce
1 teaspoon mild vinegar
2 teaspoons plain flour
2 cloves garlic, crushed

Other ingredients
3 cloves garlic, finely chopped
5-cm (2-inch) piece of fresh ginger, peeled and finely sliced
10 whole green peppercorns
10 green peppercorns, roughly crushed
3 tablespoons hot water
2 tablespoons dark soy sauce
4 spring onions, cut into thin rounds
2 tablespoons chopped flat-leaf parsley
2 tablespoons *mirin* (Japanese rice wine) or dry sherry

Put the pork in a bowl and mix in all the ingredients for the marinade. Leave to marinate for 30 minutes or longer.

Heat the oil in a wok or frying pan, and fry the mushrooms in two batches for 3 minutes each time. Take them out with a slotted spoon and put them on a plate lined with some absorbent paper. In the remaining oil fry the pork in four batches, each time for 3 minutes. Take them out with a slotted spoon and drain in a colander.

You may need to add just another tablespoon of oil to the wok or pan. Heat the oil again, then fry the chopped garlic, ginger and peppercorns, stirring all the time, for 2 minutes. Add the hot water and soy sauce, stir and add the fried meat and mushrooms. Stir them around for 1 minute, then add the rest of the ingredients. Keep stirring for 1 more minute. Taste, and adjust the seasoning. Serve hot.

Singapore Rice Noodles

The noodles used here are sold as 'rice sticks', and are available in various widths, the widest about 5 mm (¼ inch). Narrow ones are often labelled 'rice vermicelli'. They are whitish in colour, almost translucent, and they often come in 500 g packets (1 lb 2 oz). Check the cooking instructions on the packet; cooking times sometimes differ slightly. If there is no cooking time, or if the instructions are in a language unknown to you, follow the instructions below.

I have suggested some ingredients for the seafood mix, but you can buy any mixture that has been conveniently packed, either at your fishmonger or at the supermarket.

500 g (1 lb 2 oz) rice stick noodles
2.4 litres (4 pints) hot water
a large pinch of salt

For the seafood mixture
2 tablespoons groundnut oil
2 tablespoons chopped spring onions
125 g (4 oz) shelled prawns
125 g (4 oz) squid, cut into small pieces
125 g (4 oz) mussels (shelled)
  (alternatively, use 375 g (12 oz) of shelled prawns and omit the squid and mussels)
1 tablespoon light soy sauce

Other ingredients
3 tablespoons groundnut oil
1 onion, finely chopped
2 cloves of garlic, finely chopped
2 red chillies, seeded and chopped, or ½ teaspoon chilli powder
1 teaspoon grated ginger (optional)
1 teaspoon curry powder
175 g (6 oz) mangetout peas
2 tablespoons light soy sauce
salt and pepper to taste

Put the rice stick noodles, the hot water and salt in a large bowl and cover the bowl. Leave the noodles to soak; the widest require 30 minutes, narrower ones 15 minutes. Drain them into a colander and, if you are not going to use them straight away, run the cold tap over them for a few seconds to stop them cooking any longer. Make several cuts with kitchen scissors to shorten them so that they can be handled with a fork more easily.

Heat 2 tablespoons of oil in a small frying pan and stir-fry the spring onions with the seafood for 2 minutes. Add the soy sauce, stir, and remove from heat.

Heat another 2 tablespoons of oil in a large wok or a large shallow saucepan and fry the onion and garlic, stirring continuously, for 3 minutes. Add the chillies, ginger and curry powder. Stir again for 1 minute, then add the mangetout peas. Continue stir-frying for 2 minutes, then add the drained noodles together with the soy sauce. Keep stirring and tossing with a large spoon or a spatula until the noodles are hot. Now add the seafood mixture to the noodles and stir them well together. Adjust the seasoning, transfer everything to a warm plate or bowl, and serve immediately.

Yard-long Beans in Coconut Dressing

The coconut dressing here can be used for other vegetables, and is also good for dressing raw vegetables.

There are many fancy ways of serving these long beans; you *can* cut them up into 2-cm pieces, but this makes them look like any other beans. The easiest way is to bunch together 5 or 6 beans, and make them into a loose knot. One of these knots makes one serving.

625–750 g (1¼–1½ lb) yard-long beans, blanched and made into 6 knots

The coconut dressing
1 coconut, shelled, and the brown inner skin peeled away
1 teaspoon fried shrimp paste, or 1 teaspoon anchovy paste
2 cloves garlic, crushed
juice of 1 lime
½ teaspoon chilli powder
½ teaspoon soft brown sugar (optional)
1 teaspoon salt

Grate the coconut with a hand grater, or put the broken fragments of it into your food processor and process it until you get fine coconut crumbs. Put the fried shrimp paste (or the anchovy paste) on a plate and mash it with the back of a spoon. Add the crushed garlic, lime juice, chilli powder, sugar (if used) and salt. Mix well. Then add this paste mixture to the grated coconut. Mix well again, taste and add more salt if necessary.

Just before serving, boil the beans in slightly-salted water for 4–5 minutes. Drain and put them on a serving dish and sprinkle the coconut dressing on top. Alternatively coat the beans with the coconut dressing by rolling them in it until they are well covered. Serve immediately.

Pavlova with Strawberries

In the strawberry season you can afford to be generous with them, and I know of no better way of making them really special. The best strawberries, in my experience, are the ones you choose in the 'pick-your-own' strawberry field.

1 kg (2 lb) strawberries

For the pavlova
4 egg whites (size 2 eggs)
a pinch of salt
175 g (6 oz) caster sugar
1 teaspoon cornflour
1 teaspoon white distilled vinegar
600 ml (1 pint) double cream

Line a baking tray with parchment paper and draw a pencil line on it to indicate the size and shape of your meringue. It can be oval, round or heart-shaped if you wish – I just draw around the rim of the dish I am going to serve it on.

Preheat the oven to 130°C/250°F/Gas Mark ½.

Whisk the egg whites with the salt until stiff. Add half the sugar while still whipping for 2 more minutes. Mix the cornflour with the remaining sugar and fold into the mixture. Add the vinegar and mix it in gently with a metal spoon.

Spoon the mixture within the pencilled outline on the prepared baking tray and bake for 1¼ hours. Take the meringue out of the oven, put it upside-down on the serving dish, peel off the parchment paper and leave to cool.

Just before serving, beat the cream until it is thick but not too stiff, and spread it over the meringue. To serve: cut the pavlova into six portions and serve on individual plates; ask your guests to help themselves to the strawberries.

Buffet Party for
Fourteen to Sixteen

This menu is equally suitable for either an outdoor or an indoor party. The satays, of course, are ideal for grilling on charcoal out of doors. But they are just as good done in the kitchen on a gas or electric grill. Here, as with the other buffet-party menus, I have followed the Asian custom of putting a range of dishes on the table so that even very fussy eaters will find something to their taste. I am confident, though, that the great majority of your guests will come back for more of everything.

The Menu

Rice vermicelli in coconut milk soup
Sweet and sour vegetables
Seafood salad
Fried rice
Pork and lamb satays
with piquant sauce

◆

Soft fruit kissel with soft cheese fritters
Fresh fruit salad

ABOUT THE FOOD

Rice vermicelli in coconut milk soup

Soup is more often than not on the table all through the meal in a party in South-East Asia, though of course it tastes much better at the beginning, when it is still piping hot. A solution is to leave the soup tureen on an electric hotplate; then, as is customary in the East, your guests can come back to it, either in the middle of the meal or just before the dessert. The Laotians serve the vermicelli and other extras, such as different kinds of vegetables, meat and garnishes, in separate dishes on a tray; the guests put what they want into their bowls and add the hot soup at the end. The Burmese call their national soup *Mohinga*; the noodles are accompanied, most often, by seafood and the soup is quite spicy, hot and sour, like most of the Thai *Tom Yam* soups. The recipe here is the Malaysian version, except that instead of using seafood I use chicken and chicken stock, because there is already a seafood salad in the menu.

Sweet and sour vegetables

Combinations of sweet-and-sour and hot-and-sour tastes are very common in South-East Asia. This recipe is not from any particular location or country. It is another meeting of western seasonal ingredients with oriental flavours. Here I add tofu as an optional ingredient, as it is something of an acquired taste; on the other hand, it is full of nutrients necessary to a vegetarian's diet. If you have some vegetarians among the guests, this dish will be their alternative to the meat dishes. The small round aubergines can be bought in oriental shops. They have a pleasantly bitter-sweet taste, very nice raw or just lightly cooked. If they are not available do not replace them with large aubergines: either leave them out altogether or replace them with something entirely different, such as sweet peppers.

Seafood salad

Many friends have described my salad dressing for the seafood as subtle and intriguing – so I hope your guests will also be intrigued by this salad. The origin of the recipe is Thailand, though you can find a very similar dish in Bali and elsewhere in Indonesia, as well as in Malaysia and the Philippines.

Fried rice

My recipe here is a very basic one, as the fried rice is the staple for this menu – in other words, it is used as a base, on which the vegetables, fish and meat are put. For a one-dish meal, you would make a more elaborate fried rice.

Pork and lamb satays

Satay is the South-East Asian version of kebab: meat or fish cut up quite small and grilled on skewers. Satays are smaller than kebabs, however, and there is not usually any mixing of meat and vegetables on the same skewer. The skewers themselves are made of split bamboo, though you can perfectly well use metal ones. Each country has its own marinades and there are many varieties of sauces, though the best-known and probably the most popular is the savoury-spicy Peanut Sauce (page 191). The version that I give here is certainly my own favourite, and by good luck it happens to be one of the simplest and quickest to make.

Soft fruit kissel with soft cheese fritters

This is a dessert from Eastern Europe, given to me by a friend, Silvija Davidson, who is an excellent cook and loves talking about food and finding out about it as much as I do. I got the recipe in mid-December, and the first time I made it was to round off our Christmas dinner of goose with prune and apple stuffing accompanied by roast potatoes and parsnips. I made the kissel itself with cranberries, which were more or less seasonal, but it is at least as good, if not better, with the summer soft fruit.

Fresh fruit salad

In the East we always end our spicy meal with fresh fruit. At this point in the proceedings, we are not as attentive to our guests as during the main course. We just leave the fruit, whole and uncut, for people to choose what they want and eat it as they please. The good host is of course expected to make sure that all the fruit is in peak condition, and cutting it up for a fruit salad is a good way of doing that. Besides, it gives me the opportunity and excuse to add a spoonful or two of Cointreau or Grand Marnier.

PLANNING AND PREPARATION

If you are having the party out of doors, you can ask the guests to grill their own satays at the last moment, or you can grill them while guests are helping themselves to the other food. In any case, don't forget to light your charcoal in plenty of time to get the best glow when it's time to start grilling. For best results, the satays need to be marinated overnight. The cheese fritters are the only other item in this menu that will be better if fried at the last moment, though they can also be done a few minutes before your guests arrive. They will still be fresh enough to serve with the cold kissel at the end of the meal.

The day before:

Marinate the meat for the satays.
Prepare the stock for the soup.
Keep these in the fridge.

On the day:

MORNING
Make the fruit kissel and prepare the cheese mixture for the fritters. Refrigerate until required.
Prepare the seafood salad and keep in the fridge – do not add the dressing yet.
Make the piquant sauce for the satays.
Prepare the fruit salad.
Prepare ingredients for the fried rice.

EVENING – for 8.30 dinner

6.15   Cook the fried rice and keep in a heatproof dish covered tightly with aluminium foil.

6.25   Dress the seafood salad, arrange on a platter and keep in a cool place.
Make coconut milk and cook the soup but keep the vermicelli and the other ingredients on a separate dish.

6.40   Cook the sweet and sour vegetables.

6.50   Fry the cheese fritters, keep in a cool place, to be served at room temperature with the cold kissel.

8.00   Turn on oven at 150°C/300°F/Gas Mark 2.

8.10 Put the fried rice in the oven to heat for 10–15 minutes.
Heat the soup and put in a large bowl on a hot plate with the vermicelli and other ingredients and the individual soup bowls ready at hand.

8.25 Arrange everything on the table ready for the guests to help themselves.

8.30 Start grilling the satays while guests are serving themselves to other things.

Rice Vermicelli in Coconut Milk Soup

This is a very substantial soup with coconut milk added to the broth. For a large party, therefore, when there are many other dishes, you will be safe if you allow something like half a normal portion per person.

2 small chickens
2 litres (3½ pints) water
2 tablespoons vegetable oil
4 shallots, sliced
2 cloves of garlic, crushed
1 or 2 dried red chillies
1 teaspoon finely-chopped ginger
25 g (1 oz) dried shrimps, soaked in hot water for 10 minutes, then drained
½ teaspoon ground coriander
a large pinch of turmeric
250 g (8 oz) rice vermicelli
1 litre (1¾ pints) very thick coconut milk (see page 27)
salt and pepper to taste

For the garnish
250 g (8 oz) beansprouts, blanched
6 tablespoons finely-sliced spring onions
4 tablespoons chopped flat-leaf parsley
125 g (4 oz) fried onion flakes (see page 197)

Cut each chicken into four and boil the pieces in the water in a large saucepan for 45 minutes. Then take the chicken out of the pan, and separate the meat from the bones and skin. Put the chicken pieces in the fridge and put the bones and skin back into the saucepan; continue simmering while you are preparing the rest of the soup.

Heat the oil in a frying pan, and fry the shallots, garlic, chillies and ginger for 2 minutes, stirring all the time. Add the dried shrimps, the coriander and turmeric, stir again and add this mixture to the chicken stock in the pan; continue to simmer for 15 minutes. Then strain this stock through a strainer lined with muslin into another saucepan. If you make this stock a few hours or a day in advance, refrigerate it and skim off the fat before you assemble the soup, ready to serve.

Put the rice vermicelli in a large bowl and pour in enough boiling water to cover it. Cover the bowl and leave for 3 minutes, then strain off the water. Keep the vermicelli warm.

To assemble the soup, first heat the stock until it is just warm, add the coconut milk, and gently bring this to the boil. Stir, then transfer into two large bowls and put them on a hot plate. Arrange the chicken pieces, the vermicelli and all the garnishes nicely on a flat serving dish. Put this next to the soup with the individual soup bowls for the guests to help themselves. First you ask your guests to put some chicken and vermicelli with whatever garnish they fancy into their bowls, then you can ladle the soup over the top.

Sweet and Sour Vegetables

There are many vegetables that go well with this sweet and sour sauce. Feel free therefore to choose your own combination. My concern here is to have vegetables that go well together and with the rest of the dishes in the menu.

2 slim cucumbers
6 courgettes
375 g (12 oz) tofu (optional)
8–10 small round aubergines, quartered
8–10 small firm red tomatoes, quartered
1 medium-size pineapple, or 3 sour apples, peeled, cored and cut into
 cubes

For the sweet and sour sauce
2 tablespoons groundnut or olive oil
2 shallots, finely sliced
1 clove garlic, finely sliced
2 large green chillies, seeded and finely sliced
1 teaspoon finely-chopped ginger
2 tablespoons rice vinegar or white wine vinegar
1–2 teaspoons brown sugar
salt and pepper to taste

Cut the cucumbers lengthways, scoop out and discard the seeds, cut the cucumber halves into 5–6 pieces and then into thickish sticks about 2 cm (¾ inch) in length. Do the same with the courgettes.

If using tofu, put it in a bowl and pour boiling water to cover it. Leave standing for 8–10 minutes. Then drain, and cut into 16 cubes.

Heat the oil in a wok or a large shallow saucepan, and fry the shallots, garlic and chillies for 2 minutes, stirring all the time. Add the rest of the ingredients for the sauce. Simmer gently for 2–3 minutes. Now add the rest of the ingredients. Stir – carefully, if you are using tofu, so as not to break it up too much. Cover the wok or pan and continue to simmer for 3 more minutes. Uncover, adjust the seasoning and serve hot or cold.

Seafood Salad

Everything needs to be really fresh for this seafood salad, so choose whatever is best among the fish available on the day. Just as a guideline, a possible and very good combination is: lobster or king prawns, squid and two other fish, such as tuna and salmon.

For the salad
1 cooked lobster or 500 g (1 lb) king prawns, poached for 3 minutes and
    peeled
500 g (1 lb) small squid, cut into rings and poached for 3 minutes
250 g (8 oz) tuna steak, poached for 3 minutes
250 g (8 oz) salmon steak, poached for 3 minutes
125 g (4 oz) crispy lettuce leaves
125 g (4 oz) radicchio
10 coriander leaves

For the dressing
2 small red chillies, seeded and finely chopped
5-cm (2-inch) piece of lemon grass, outer leaves discarded, then finely
    chopped
2 fresh kaffir lime leaves, finely shredded
2 tablespoons fish sauce (*nam pla*)
3 tablespoons chopped spring onions
2 tablespoons lime or lemon juice
2 tablespoons mild vinegar
2 teaspoons caster sugar

If using lobster, slice it into small bite-sized pieces. If using king prawns, cut them in two lengthwise. Cut the fish into small bite-sized pieces.

Mix the dressing well, and dress the seafood 30 minutes before serving.

To serve: arrange the salad leaves with the coriander leaves on a plate and pile the dressed seafood on top.

Fried Rice

This is only one of many variations of fried rice. This particular recipe is good for freezing, so for this party you can make it a day before or a week ahead. Or make a lot on the day, and freeze the left-overs. Allow at least half a cup of cooked rice per person.

10 cups of plain cooked rice (page 25)
2 tablespoons groundnut or olive oil
1 tablespoon butter
4 shallots, finely sliced
2 cloves of garlic, finely sliced
2 red chillies, seeded and finely chopped, or ½ teaspoon chilli powder
2 tablespoons light soy sauce
1 teaspoon paprika
2 teaspoons tomato purée
250 g (8 oz) button mushrooms, cleaned and sliced
4 medium-size carrots, peeled and diced
salt to taste

Heat the oil and butter in a wok or a large shallow saucepan. Fry the shallots, garlic and chillies for 2 minutes, then add the other ingredients, and stir-fry for 5 minutes or more until the vegetables are cooked. Then add the rice, and mix it well with the vegetables by stirring continuously until the rice is hot. Taste, and add salt or more soy sauce if necessary. Serve hot.

Pork and Lamb Satays with Piquant Sauce

For best results, marinate the meat overnight and put the pieces on the skewers the next day. If using bamboo skewers, soak them first in cold water for a few hours, then wash them well. This is to prevent them catching fire on the charcoal. Here I give an alternative piquant sauce to the usual peanut sauce. However, you will find the traditional recipe for peanut sauce on page 191.

625 g (1¼ lb) tenderloin of pork, cut into 2-cm (¾-inch) cubes
625 g (1¼ lb) lamb leg meat, cut into 2-cm (¾-inch) cubes

For the marinade
8 shallots, peeled and finely sliced
4 cloves garlic, peeled and finely sliced
3 teaspoons ground coriander
1 teaspoon ground cumin
½ teaspoon chilli powder
¾ teaspoon coarsely-ground black pepper
1 teaspoon finely-chopped ginger

3 tablespoons light soy sauce
1 tablespoon groundnut or olive oil
1 tablespoon white distilled malt vinegar or lemon juice
½ teaspoon salt
2 teaspoons brown sugar

Mix well all the ingredients for the marinade. Divide it equally between two bowls. Marinate the pork pieces in one bowl and the lamb in the other. Keep in the fridge overnight.

Just before grilling, put the meat on bamboo skewers, 4 or 5 pieces of meat to each skewer. Grill for 3 minutes on one side, turn them over and continue grilling for at least another 2 minutes for the lamb and 3 minutes for the pork.

For the piquant sauce
3 fresh small chillies, finely chopped, or ½ tsp chilli powder
4 cloves garlic, peeled and finely chopped
1 teaspoon sugar
2 tablespoons white distilled vinegar
2 tablespoons light soy sauce
2 tablespoons hot water
1 tablespoon olive oil
4 tablespoons coarsely-ground roasted or fried peanuts

Mix all the ingredients for the sauce in a glass bowl and serve as a dip with the hot satays.

Soft Fruit Kissel with Soft Cheese Fritters

Silvija Davidson, who gave me this Latvian recipe, says 'the kissel is made most traditionally with wild cranberries and potato flour, though many variants exist'. She suggested that for the summer the kissel should be made with blackcurrants and redcurrants. I myself haven't found it necessary to add any flour at all.

500 g (1 lb) blackcurrants
500 g (1 lb) redcurrants
200 g (7 oz) caster sugar
2 level teaspoons arrowroot or 2 rounded teaspoons potato flour (optional)

Crush the fruit lightly with a pestle and press it gently in a nylon sieve to extract the juice. Keep the juice aside. Place the fruit pulp with the sugar and 450 ml (¾ pint) water in a saucepan. Bring to the boil, then simmer gently, stirring from time to time, for 5 minutes. Strain through a nylon sieve into a second bowl, pressing down hard on the pulp. Rinse out the saucepan and place it in the juice from the cooked fruit. Dissolve the arrowroot/potato flour (if used) in a little cold water and stir it into the juice in the pan. Bring it to the boil once more, stirring constantly, and simmer gently for a further 3 minutes until glossy, thick and clear. Allow to cool a little, then mix together both juices and check for sweetness, adding a further spoonful or two of sugar to taste. Serve hot or cool.

For the fritters
500 g (1 lb) well-drained fromage blanc or very fresh ricotta
2 tablespoons caster sugar
a few drops genuine vanilla essence
½ teaspoon finely-grated lemon zest
1 teaspoon lemon juice (optional)
a small pinch of salt
1 large egg, beaten
4–6 tablespoons sifted plain flour
a little unsalted butter for frying
extra caster sugar and 8 or more tablespoons of thick crème fraîche and a
    dusting of cinnamon, to serve

Beat or sieve the cheese until no lumps remain. Beat in the sugar and vanilla, lemon zest, lemon juice if used and salt. Blend in the egg, then beat in the flour, a spoonful at a time, to give a mouldable consistency. (Fromage blanc will probably require all the flour, whilst ricotta may need only four spoonsful.)

Chill for half an hour or more, if time allows. For a particularly neat end result, the cheese can be chilled in a fat sausage shape, rolled up in wax paper. Slice the sausage into 24 rounds, or form the unrolled mixture into 24 neat patties. Brush a cast-iron griddle or heavy frying pan with a little butter, and heat until fairly hot before arranging the fritters in the pan. Cook for 2–3 minutes each side, turning them over once with a nylon spatula, until golden brown.

Serve at once, if possible, sprinkled with a little extra sugar, surrounded by kissel, and with a dollop of cream and a dusting of cinnamon. The fritters can also be served in a separate bowl from the kissel.

Fresh Fruit Salad

I always find a fresh fruit salad a very useful standby for any dinner party. In this menu, it is necessary as the kissel and cheese fritters will serve full portions for twelve people at most. You may already have your own favourite fruit salad recipe – but if you want to try mine, I don't think you will be disappointed.

Mix the fruit juice in a large glass bowl first, before you start cutting up the rest of the fruit. You can then put the cut-up fruit straight into the juice to prevent discoloration – particularly important for apples.

For the juice
juice of 2 large oranges
juice of 4 passion fruits
juice of 1 lime
2 tablespoons caster sugar (optional)

The rest of the fruit
3 red apples, washed, cored, quartered and thinly sliced, and put straight
 into the juice in the bowl
500 g (1 lb) strawberries, washed, the large ones cut in half
3 large oranges, peeled and segmented
1 ripe papaya, peeled, seeded and cut into small cubes
2 pink grapefruits, peeled and segmented

Mix all the fruit in the bowl with the juice. Chill until needed.

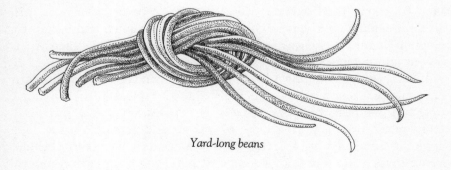

Yard-long beans

Autumn

MOST PEOPLE in the world are still farmers – or at most they're only two or three generations away from the land. Wherever we come from, we retain some memory of the two events that regulate our lives, sowing and harvest. I have mentioned in another book the rice-dolls that Asian farmers still make to preserve the soul of the rice after the crop has been cut, and the corn-dollies that were made on English farms for a similar purpose until quite recently. In Indonesia, Dewi Sri is the goddess of rice, which is probably why there are as many girls called Sri as there are Marys or Maries in Europe and America. Not long ago I had lunch at a farm in Berkshire, and sat opposite the farmer's young daughter. She told me her name, which I didn't catch at first but which turned out to be Ceres. How appropriate for a farmer's daughter to be named after the old Mediterranean corn goddess, and how unusual! She pronounced it with the first syllable short and the second much longer, so that the similarity of her name and mine was obvious. Could they, indeed, be the same name, originating perhaps in India when men (or more likely women) were learning to be farmers, or is this another example of the false etymology which is such a temptation to amateur linguists? Anyway, we two goddesses congratulated each other on our unusual meeting.

In fact, what I look forward to in late summer and autumn is the fruit, particularly figs and plums, which are almost tropical in their plumpness and juiciness. I love apples too, but apples, crisp and shiny, are temperate fruit which I associate with Celts and Scandinavians. The apple, in Greek mythology, that Paris awarded as first prize in a beauty contest was really, I'm told, a quince. When I was first married and we were still living in Yogyakarta, in Central Java, a friend of ours went on leave to England and brought back as a present for my husband a big glossy green cooking apple that she had picked in an orchard in Kent two days before. In a country where – at that time – the only apples were eight hours' drive away, in Surabaya or Jakarta, and were frozen Californian apples that tasted like cotton-wool, this showed a real genius for present-giving. An American friend taught me how to make pastry and I baked my first apple pie, not at all bad, though a tropical climate is not ideal for pastry. I must add that you can get very good apples in Indonesia today, because the demand for them now makes it worth while to ship fresh Australian fruit at reasonable prices. Importing fruit to a tropical island may seem a bit like carrying snow to the North Pole, but it is precisely this availability of any kind of food, anywhere, at any season, that makes the menus in this book accessible to everyone. I have to admit, though, that some of my ingredients (mascarpone cheese, for example) would probably seem more exotic and be harder to find in Jakarta than galingale is in London or New York.

The kind friend who brought my husband the apple was, in her way, a typical member of the foreign academic community in Yogyakarta in those days; the daughter of a well-to-do Jewish family in Moscow, she had danced with the Bolshoi, departed from Russia after the revolution and married an ebullient nuclear physicist whose father had been a member of the Jewish community in Syria. Needless to say, they were by far the most English of the overseas community. Almost every nationality had its representatives, and as they were all academics they contained a ripe crop of individuals and eccentrics. They knew they were having the time of their lives – the men, at any rate. European women had too little to do and some found leisure a burden. Not surprisingly, there was some very interesting cooking being done and some memorable meals were produced.

A Japanese lecturer asked my husband to help his wife with her English. Teacher and pupil strove valiantly for several sessions with syntax and pronunciation but eventually we all gave up and went to their house for sukiyaki, cooked in front of us by the husband, who also kept pouring glass after glass of Johnnie Walker for the men while his wife poured green tea for the ladies. Another household with a great regard for whisky was that of our Russian next-door neighbours. They would summon us to have a drink at sunset on their verandah, as was the local custom, and would then refuse to let us go, virtually imprisoning us until we had eaten an enormous dinner washed down, not with vodka because they could get that at home, but good single malt. As they came from different republics of the USSR, they made great play with the fact that their marriage was a mixed one, like ours, and every meal had to have a full range of dishes from both their homelands.

I occasionally get asked about major influences on my career as a cook. The main one has been that I simply enjoy food and am always looking out for new dishes. If I eat something at a friend's house or a restaurant that I particularly like, I can usually recreate it for myself later. For people who don't enjoy cooking this may seem like black magic, but it is similar to a musician's ability to play by ear – it is just a matter of experience. I've dedicated this book to the memory of my father's mother, whose kitchen I always regard as the place from which I really set out into life. My father was a good cook, too. He was not very complimentary about his daughters' talents in the kitchen, and when I was engaged I felt bound to warn my fiancé that cooking was out; I had often been told I was hopeless at it. I suppose I owe him something for staying loyal to me in the face of such an admission. By the time I arrived in England, eighteen months later, I had become quite an experienced dinner-party giver on the local circuit; we used to invite ten or a dozen people and deliberately mix them up as much as possible, scientists with historians, atheists with Jesuits. They regarded Central Java as neutral ground anyway. We even invited young people with much older ones, which in the sixties was considered daring.

Looking back, I think I already knew how I was going to develop. I knew I liked Italian food, and this was reinforced when we sailed from Asia on an Italian ship called Asia and Italy became my first experience of Europe. I love France too, but I have never felt as close to it as I do to the southern Mediterranean countries; I have paid brief visits to Spain and Yugoslavia, to my regret I have never been to Greece, but I feel I know these places through their cooking and they have certainly influenced mine. Much the same goes for the Middle East, where of course I begin to recognise familiar landmarks because Arab traders brought so many of their traditions to Indonesia and converted my people to Islam. Between Europe and Asia lies Turkey, and in recent years I have absorbed more ideas and techniques from Turkey than perhaps anywhere else, largely as a result of two visits to food conferences sponsored by the Turkish Ministry of Tourism. In all these countries, mass marketing of food is taking its hold. It would be encouraging to think that one day people who call themselves independent will realise that standardised food products are another form of colonialism and will reject them. Meanwhile, exchanging ideas in the kitchen and eating each other's food seems to me like a more real kind of internationalism.

Dinner for Four

This is one of those meals where the dishes look and sound impressive but are actually quite simple to prepare. One pays a price, of course, for simplicity; mistakes are harder to hide. But there is no reason why you should have any difficulties with these recipes. Between the rice and potatoes, I think I would choose the rice, more often than not; I hope my readers all know how to cook perfect rice by now, and that is something many people are impressed by.

The Menu

Vietnamese noodle soup with steamed duck

◆

Clear-steamed sea bass
served with
Plain boiled rice or potatoes
and
Stuffed Chinese mushrooms
Stir-fried spinach

◆

Poppyseed parfait with plum sauce

ABOUT THE FOOD

Vietnamese noodle soup with steamed duck

There is nothing especially Vietnamese in this soup; most noodle soups in South-East Asia are pretty similar because they all originated in China. Like the Malaysian noodle soup with coconut milk, this is usually made with rice noodles or so-called rice sticks; here we use the wide ribbon kind rather than the vermicelli.

Clear-steamed sea bass

This is in my opinion absolutely the best way of cooking sea bass; it is a recipe from Yan-kit So's *Classic Chinese Cookbook* (Dorling Kindersley, 1984), which is also one of the best books on Chinese cooking.

Boiled rice

Although there are fancier ways to cook rice, some of which are described elsewhere in this book, I think that plain boiled rice, or boiled potatoes, will set off the other dishes in this menu better than anything else.

Stuffed Chinese mushrooms

The uncomplicated way of cooking the sea bass suggests a richer accompaniment: hence these stuffed mushrooms. Again this is a recipe from Yan-kit So's *Classic Chinese Cookbook*. If you find the entire menu is a little too much, use these stuffed mushrooms as the first course, served on their own or with a small salad, and leave out the soup altogether. If you make the soup some other time, the quantity shown here will be just right for lunch or a late supper for two people.

Stir-fried spinach

Don't feel that you have to stir-fry your spinach if you prefer to cook it some other way. It is the spinach that matters, not how it is cooked; but stir-frying is quick and convenient, and preserves texture and flavour.

Poppyseed parfait with plum sauce

Another 'borrowed' dessert that will certainly go well with the oriental flavour of the menu. It is from the *Gidleigh Park Cookery Book* (Century, 1990), written by Gidleigh's famous chef, Shaun Hill.

PLANNING AND PREPARATION

Make the parfait the day before, and on the morning of the party do everything else that can be done in advance: stuff the mushrooms, clean the spinach and the fish, and prepare all the chopped and sliced ingredients. Thirty minutes will be ample for the last-minute preparation in the evening before the guests arrive. The soup is ready to heat up at a second's notice, and you can leave the mushrooms steaming while you are enjoying the soup. The fish can be cooked after the soup course is over, as can everything else that remains to be done for the main course.

The day before:

Make the parfait and freeze.

On the day:

MORNING
Prepare and steam the duck for the soup and make the stock.
Prepare all the rest of the ingredients.
Prepare the fish, and slice the spring onions and ginger.
Prepare and stuff the mushrooms.
Keep all these in the fridge.
Wash the spinach, drain well and keep wrapped in a tea-towel in the fridge.

EVENING – for 8.30 dinner

8.00   Assemble the soup ingredients and heat the stock on a very low heat.

8.10   Get ready lots of boiling water to steam the mushrooms and fish. Start cooking rice or potatoes.

8.20   Steam the mushrooms and heat the sauce.

8.30   SERVE THE SOUP

8.45   Steam the fish.
Arrange the mushrooms on a serving dish and pour the sauce over them.

Put the rice or potatoes in a serving bowl.

8.50   Transfer the fish from the steamer to a serving dish – spread the spring onions and ginger on it. Heat the oil and pour over fish. Stir-fry the spinach.

9.00   Transfer the parfait from the freezer to the fridge.
        SERVE THE MAIN COURSE

Vietnamese Noodle Soup with Steamed Duck

If you have been waiting for a chance to cook the legs of a duck into something interesting, here is your opportunity; though you can, if you prefer, make this soup with breast fillets. Use chicken stock or vegetable stock, not duck stock.

2 whole legs of duck or 2 breast fillets
300 ml (½ pint) groundnut or corn oil

For the marinade
2 tablespoons dark soy sauce
1 tablespoon fish sauce
¼ teaspoon chilli powder
¼ teaspoon ground coriander
½ teaspoon five-spice powder
1 tablespoon clear honey
1 teaspoon grated ginger

For the noodle soup
1.2 litres (2 pints) water
a pinch of salt
125 g (4 oz) rice-stick noodles
600 ml (1 pint) chicken or vegetable stock
125 g (4 oz) pak choy or Chinese cabbage, roughly chopped
2 tablespoons chopped spring onions
2 tablespoons chopped coriander leaves
salt and pepper to taste

Mix all the ingredients for the marinade in a glass bowl, and marinate the duck for at least 2 hours or overnight.

Drain the duck pieces from the marinade. Put them on a plate and steam them, over boiling water and a very high heat, in a wok or saucepan (see page 28) for 20 minutes. Leave them to cool, then fry them in hot oil for 5–6 minutes. Drain and keep aside.

Heat the water for the soup in a large saucepan, and when boiling add the pinch of salt and the rice-stick noodles. Simmer for 2 minutes, drain the noodles in a colander and put them under a cold running tap for a minute or so to stop them cooking.

Rinse the large saucepan, pour the stock into it and bring it to the boil. Add the rest of the ingredients for the soup, except the noodles and coriander leaves, and season to taste. Simmer for 2 minutes. In the meantime, slice the duck meat off the bones. Divide the noodles among four bowls, top them with equal amounts of sliced meat, and when you are ready to eat, pour the soup into the bowls. Sprinkle with the coriander leaves. Serve straight away.

Clear-steamed Sea Bass

1 sea bass, 700 g–1.2 kg (1½–2½ lb), cleaned and with head left on
¼ teaspoon salt
¼ teaspoon sugar
2 teaspoons finely-chopped or grated ginger
5–7 spring onions, cut into very fine julienne strips
2–3 tablespoons groundnut or sunflower oil
2–3 tablespoons light soy sauce

Pat the fish dry. Make 2 or 3 diagonal slashes on both sides of the fish. Lay the fish on a heatproof serving dish with slightly raised sides. If your wok or steamer is rather small the fish can be halved, and the halves put side by side on a round plate.

Steam in a wok or steamer, covered, over a high heat for about 8 minutes until the fish is cooked and the flesh flakes easily. Remove the cover, reduce the heat. If too much water from the steam has collected on the plate, use kitchen paper to absorb some of it.

Sprinkle the fish with salt and sugar. Spread the ginger and then the spring onions on the fish. Heat the oil in a small saucepan over a high heat until smoke rises. Pour it little by little over the spring onions and ginger. The sizzling oil partially cooks them, enhancing the flavour.

Remove the dish from the wok or steamer. Add the soy sauce and serve immediately.

Stuffed Chinese Mushrooms

The dried mushrooms used here need to be reconstituted before being stuffed. Rinse them, then put them in a bowl and pour on boiling water to cover them. Cover the bowl with a plate, and leave the mushrooms soaking in the water for 30 minutes. Cut the stalks off and reserve them for the stock pot. Keep the soaking water for use in the sauce.

16–20 thick or medium dried Chinese mushrooms, or Japanese shiitake, reconstituted
50 g (2 oz) lean pork
3 water chestnuts, finely chopped
4 spring onions, cut into thin rounds
1 tablespoon groundnut or corn oil

For the marinade
1 teaspoon finely-chopped ginger
a large pinch of salt
½ teaspoon sugar
2 teaspoons light soy sauce
¼ teaspoon ground white pepper
1 teaspoon Shaohsing wine or dry sherry
½ teaspoon potato flour
1 tablespoon water
1 egg white

For the sauce
1½ teaspoons potato flour, dissolved in 1 tablespoon cold water
175 ml (6 fl oz) mushroom water
1 tablespoon oyster sauce
1 tablespoon dark soy sauce
2 tablespoons groundnut or corn oil

Chop the pork by hand or mince it coarsely and put it into a bowl.

Mix all the ingredients for the marinade, except the egg white, into the pork. With a wooden spoon, stir the contents of the bowl, always in the same direction, for about 1 minute. Add the egg white and stir again in the same direction for 30 seconds or until the mixture is smooth and light. Leave to marinate for about 15 minutes. Then mix in the chopped water chestnuts and the spring onions together with 1 tablespoon of oil. The stuffing is now ready.

Drain and squeeze out the excess water from the mushrooms but leave them damp. Reserve the soaking liquid. Hold a mushroom cap in one hand with the hollow side up and using a small knife fill the hollow generously with the stuffing, shaping it into a gently-sloping little hill so that it has an attractive appearance. Repeat until all are done. Put them on a heatproof dish, stuffing side up, in one layer. You can do everything up to this point on the morning of the dinner party.

Just before you are ready to serve the main course, put the dish in a wok or steamer and steam, tightly covered, over a high heat for 10 minutes. A few minutes before the end of the steaming time, put all the ingredients for the sauce except the oil in a small saucepan. Bring it to the boil, then stir continuously until it becomes thick. Blend in the oil, which will give the sauce a sheen. Remove the mushrooms from the steamer. Arrange them in two layers in the same heatproof dish or on a warm serving dish and pour the sauce over them. Serve piping hot.

Stir-fried Spinach

700 g (1½ lb) spinach, washed
1 tablespoon vegetable oil
3 shallots or 1 small onion, finely sliced
3 cloves garlic, finely sliced
1 teaspoon finely-sliced ginger
a pinch of ground or grated nutmeg
salt and pepper to taste

Drain the spinach well after it has been washed.

Heat the oil in a wok or large saucepan and stir-fry the shallots, garlic and ginger for 1 minute. Add the spinach and continue stir-frying for 2–3 minutes more. Season with the nutmeg, salt and pepper. Transfer the spinach with the cooking juices onto a hot serving plate and serve immediately.

Poppyseed Parfait with Plum Sauce

I have reproduced Shaun Hill's recipe for this delicious parfait with his permission.

You don't need an ice-cream machine for this frozen dessert. The ideal container for freezing the parfait is an oblong Pyrex dish measuring about 11.5 × 23 cm (4½ × 9 in). For best results, the parfait need only be in the freezer until it is frozen (about 3–4 hours), but for this menu I recommend making the parfait the day before the party so that you have plenty of time to concentrate on preparing and cooking everything else.

For the parfait
4 egg yolks
100 g (4 oz) caster sugar
1 tablespoon honey
250 ml (8 fl oz) milk
1 vanilla pod
400 ml (14 fl oz) double cream
50 g (2 oz) poppyseed

For the plum sauce
450 g (1 lb) red plums
225 g (8 oz) granulated sugar
juice of ½ lemon
300 ml (10 fl oz) water

Make a *sabayon* with the egg yolks, sugar and honey. Do this by whisking the ingredients together over a very low heat until the mixture cooks, first fluffing up and then thickening, without scrambling the egg.

In a small saucepan, bring the milk and vanilla pod to the boil, then strain. Whisk the hot flavoured milk into the *sabayon*, then leave to cool.

Whip the cream and then fold it, with the poppyseeds, into the *sabayon* and milk mixture. Spoon this mixture into the Pyrex dish and freeze until required.

To make the plum sauce: put the plums, sugar, lemon juice and water into a saucepan. Bring them to the boil, cover, and simmer for 10 minutes. Pick out the stones and liquidise the plums and the juice together in a blender. Leave to cool.

To serve the parfait, turn it out of the dish. (Dip the dish into warm water for a few seconds, then turn it upside down.) Slice the parfait about 2.5 cm (1 in) thick, put a slice (or two) on each plate, and pour the sauce all round it but not over it. Alternatively, put the sauce in a jug and let your guests help themselves.

Dinner for Six

Many of my guests would regard this as the most exotic of the three autumn menus. Try it for just six people to begin with. Once you feel confident preparing the phoenix rolls, and as long as you do not mind spending more than an hour making the rice sorbet, I recommend this menu for much larger parties. The last-minute preparation is easy. Just double or treble the quantities of ingredients shown here, as appropriate. You don't need to fry the phoenix rolls at the very last moment, or serve them piping hot straight from the wok, because they are equally good warm or cold. The sorbet can stay in the freezer for several days or a week beforehand. I do hope you will try the glutinous rice, especially if you have not had it before, as an accompaniment to the main course, because I think you will find it very good – but if it doesn't appeal to you, by all means use ordinary rice or potatoes, cooked in whatever way you prefer. Incidentally, this rice is only called 'glutinous' because it is sticky – it does not contain any gluten whatsoever.

The Menu

Phoenix rolls

◆

Venison in rich coconut sauce
with
Steamed glutinous rice
and
Broccoli stir-fried with chillies and leeks

◆

Black glutinous rice sorbet

ABOUT THE FOOD

Phoenix rolls

You may well wonder what is in these rolls and why they have this name. In fact, this is a very common way in the East of cooking prawn paste. The minced prawns are mixed with pork fat, white fish or chicken, depending on what background you come from. The Chinese, Thais, Filipinos and Vietnamese all use pork fat, while the Muslim people of Malaysia and Indonesia use fish or chicken. The prawn paste mixture itself is perhaps better known as the paste used to make 'prawn toasts' and other delicate Chinese and South-East Asian snacks which are always popular with drinks (recipes on page 154).

The rolls have different names and different recipes in different countries, but I like the Chinese name and this recipe is certainly the best. It is taken from Yan-kit So's *Wok Cookbook*, published by Piatkus (1985). In her introduction to the recipe, Yan-kit wrote: 'These rolls undoubtedly belong to the realm of Chinese *haute cuisine*, involving multi-process cooking and cookery technique. The end result is one of grand simplicity, well deserving the accolade of the name "phoenix", the emblem of royalty and beauty in traditional China.'

Venison in rich coconut sauce

This is a Laotian dish. I found the original recipe in *Traditional Recipes of Laos* by Phia Sing, published by Prospect Books in 1981. The meat used there, deer meat, is not quite the same as the venison available in the West. But I have used cuts from the saddle or haunch with very satisfactory results.

Steamed glutinous rice

The Laotians, more often than their neighbours in other countries, eat plain steamed glutinous rice as an accompaniment to a savoury main course dish. The Indonesians prefer their glutinous rice cooked in coconut milk until it is quite soft, while the Thais will sweeten it and eat it with fresh fruit, such as mango, jackfruit, or the famous durian.

Broccoli stir-fried with chillies and leeks

Regarding this dish, I have nothing to add to what is written in the recipe, except to say that you can also prepare it on the morning of the dinner party, and reheat it for just a few minutes before serving.

Black glutinous rice sorbet

In the Far East, black glutinous rice is used in making porridge and other sweet snacks, eaten usually at teatime, or whenever you feel a little peckish. As a rule we don't eat pudding after lunch or dinner; our dessert, if we have any at all, is just fresh fruit. But in England, I have served black glutinous porridge, made very creamy with coconut cream, as a pudding, and my guests seem to like it. However, after trying both a number of times, I find the sorbet is even more popular.

PLANNING AND PREPARATION

As with the other menus, I suggest you cook on the day of the party and shop the day before. I would also advise making the dessert the day before. Once you are familiar with the dishes, you will probably want to multiply the numbers of your guests and therefore the quantities. This will affect the time needed for preparation, and larger pans will take longer to come to the boil; but although the exact timing will be different, you will not find that the total time required is much greater.

The day before:

Make the sorbet and freeze it.

On the day:

MORNING

Make phoenix rolls ready for frying in the evening. Keep in a cool place.
Prepare the broccoli and the rest of the ingredients.
Prepare the coconut milk for the meat. Keep all these in the fridge until required.

EVENING – for 8.15 dinner

6.00 Take everything out of the fridge. Soak the glutinous rice.
   Cook the venison ready to reheat at the last moment.
   Fry the phoenix rolls. Keep warm.

7.00   Drain the rice in a colander.
8.00   Stir-fry the broccoli and keep warm.
        Cook the glutinous rice.
8.15   SERVE THE FIRST COURSE
8.30   Reheat the venison. Transfer everything into serving dishes.
8.35   Transfer the sorbet from the freezer to the fridge.
        SERVE THE MAIN COURSE

Phoenix Rolls

As a first course I like to slice these rolls and serve them on a bed of salad leaves dressed with vinaigrette. But the rolls can also be served on their own, with a sweet chilli sauce (recipe on page 196).

For the prawn paste
300 g (10 oz) uncooked prawns without shells
½ teaspoon salt
1 teaspoon cornflour
1 egg white
50 g (2 oz) pork fat, minced
5 water chestnuts (fresh or canned), peeled and minced

For the pancakes
2 large eggs (size 1)
2 teaspoons cornflour, mixed with 2 teaspoons cold water to make a paste
a pinch of salt
1 tablespoon vegetable oil

Other ingredients
2 spring onions, 18–20 cm long (7½–8 inches)
1 egg white, lightly beaten
2 egg yolks, well beaten
cornflour
vegetable oil for deep frying

First, prepare the prawn paste. Thaw out the prawns completely, if frozen, and wash them, then pat them dry with kitchen paper. Mince them by hand or put them in a food processor. Transfer them to a large glass bowl. Add the salt, and stir with a wooden spoon, always turning in the same direction until it becomes difficult to continue. Sprinkle with the cornflour, add the egg white and stir again vigorously for 1–2 minutes or until the paste is light and fluffy in texture. Add the pork fat and minced water chestnuts and stir well to mix. Leave the paste in the refrigerator, covered, for 30 minutes or longer.

Now, make the pancakes. Beat the eggs in a bowl for 1 minute, then add the cornflour paste and continue beating until the cornflour is well mixed in. Season this batter with salt. Heat a 24-cm (9-inch) frying pan, preferably non-stick, over a moderate heat until hot. Add 1 tablespoon of oil, swirl it around to reach the sides of the pan, then pour off half of the oil into a small bowl, to be used for the next pancake. Pour in half of the batter, and tip the pan, making sure the batter covers the bottom and reaches the edges in one even layer. Fry over a low heat until the batter is set but not brown. Carefully loosen the edges with a spatula, flip the pancake over and cook the other side for 1 minute. Remove to a flat plate to cool. Repeat the process for the rest of the batter.

Divide the prawn paste into two equal portions. Spread one portion by hand evenly over half of one pancake, stopping just short of the edge. Place one spring onion across the centre of the pancake next to the prawn paste. Using a pastry brush or your fingers, smear beaten egg white on the other half of the pancake, going right to the edge. Starting with the half with the prawn paste, roll the pancake up to make a nice sausage shape. The egg white will seal the roll. Repeat this process to make the other phoenix roll.

Put the two phoenix rolls on a lightly oiled heatproof dish and steam in the wok for 10–12 minutes. Remove from the dish and let them cool for a few minutes. Wash and dry the wok.

Brush each roll with the egg yolk. Spread some cornflour on a large flat plate, and roll the phoenix rolls, one at a time, over the cornflour until evenly coated. Shake off excess flour if necessary. (Up to this point the rolls can be prepared several hours in advance.) Keep the rolls in a cool place until you are ready to deep-fry them in a wok.

To fry the phoenix rolls, half-fill the wok or a deep frying pan with oil. Heat the oil until quite hot, then carefully put the rolls into the hot oil, and deep-fry them for 4 minutes or until golden brown, turning them over twice. Remove with a large perforated strainer, then immerse them in the oil again for 10–20 seconds to crisp them further. Remove and put them on kitchen paper.

Serve warm or cold. Cut the rolls diagonally into pieces about 2.5 cm (1 inch) thick. Allow three slices per person.

Venison in Rich Coconut Sauce

The Lao name for this dish, *Khoua Sin Fahn*, means simply 'fried deer meat'. My recipe translates the original instructions, in Phia Sing's *Traditional Recipes of Laos*, into a more practical method but with the same end result. Notice that in this case we use two extractions of coconut milk (see page 28).

For the meat
1.05 kg (2½ lb) venison, from the saddle or haunch

Cut the meat into 2.5-cm (1-inch) cubes. Then rub these with ½ teaspoon of salt and 2 crushed cloves of garlic. Keep in a cool place.

For the paste
3 dried red chillies, soaked in hot water until soft (about 5 or 6 minutes)
5 shallots, peeled and roughly chopped
3 kaffir lime leaves
4 tablespoons thick coconut milk (from the first extraction; see page 28)

Liquidise these to a smooth paste.

To be added later
2 tablespoons chopped spring onions (the green part only)
salt and pepper to taste
300 ml (½ pint) second extraction coconut milk

Pour the first extraction of the coconut milk into a medium-sized saucepan; bring it to the boil and continue boiling on a high heat for 30 minutes. By this time the coconut milk will have separated into a thick white substance and a thinner liquid. Add the paste to this liquid, and continue cooking for 30 minutes, stirring it often. Now the thinner liquid has become oil and the thick substance has become golden in colour. Put in the pieces of meat. Keep the heat high and stir the meat several times while it fries in the oil for 5 minutes.

At the same time as you add the paste to the first saucepan, boil the second extraction of the coconut milk in another saucepan so that, when the meat has had 5 minutes' cooking, the thin coconut milk will have reduced almost by half. Pour the hot coconut milk into the meat saucepan, and continue cooking, stirring all the time, for 4–5 minutes. Add the chopped spring onions, and salt and pepper to taste. The meat and sauce are now ready to serve hot with sticky rice.

Steamed Glutinous Rice

Do not be surprised to see the cooked rice rather sticky; the Laotians normally eat it by hand, forming the rice into a small ball and dipping it into the sauce as you would dip a piece of bread.

500 g (1 lb) white glutinous rice, soaked in cold water for 1 hour
750 ml (1¼ pints) water

Drain the rice, put it in a saucepan, and add the water. Bring it to the boil, stir, and simmer until all the water has been absorbed. Transfer the rice to a steamer or a double saucepan, and steam it for 10 minutes. You can also steam the rice in a bamboo steamer (picture on page 150). Transfer the rice to a bowl or a serving plate, and let your guests help themselves.

You can boil the rice well in advance. Put it into the steamer, but don't start to steam it until 10 minutes before you are ready to serve the main course.

Broccoli Stir-fried with Chillies and Leeks

Not everybody likes leeks, but I recommend this combination to those who do. You can always replace this vegetable dish with another if you prefer.

1.25–1.5 kg (3–3½ lb) broccoli, cut into florets
3 tablespoons olive oil
500 g (1 lb) leeks, washed and cut into thick rounds
2–3 large red chillies, seeded and finely sliced
2.5-cm (1-inch) piece of fresh ginger, peeled and finely chopped
2 tablespoons light soy sauce
6 tablespoons cold water

Blanch the broccoli for 2 minutes and refresh it under running cold water. Leave it to drain in a colander.

Heat the oil in a large saucepan, and fry the leeks, chillies and ginger for 3 minutes, stirring them all the time. Add the soy sauce and water, and simmer, stirring often, until all the water has been absorbed. If you are doing this far in advance, take the pan off the heat and leave in a cool place. When you are ready to serve the main course, heat the leeks in the saucepan for 2 minutes, stirring all the time, and add the blanched broccoli. Stir again for another minute or until it becomes hot. Adjust the seasoning and serve immediately.

Black Glutinous Rice Sorbet

Black glutinous rice is available in most Chinese, Japanese and Thai grocery shops. Before making the sorbet, you will need to make the porridge described below. The longer you soak the rice, the quicker the cooking time will be.

75 g (3 oz) black glutinous rice, soaked for 2–8 hours, then drained
1.75 litres (3 pints) coconut milk, made from 300 g (10 oz) desiccated
    coconut
½ teaspoon salt
1 small stick of cinnamon
3 tablespoons brown sugar

To be added later
2 tablespoons glucose

Put the rice and coconut milk in a saucepan, add the salt and cinnamon stick and bring to the boil. Simmer slowly for 10 minutes, then add the sugar. Continue to simmer, stirring often, until the porridge becomes thick. The whole cooking time will be 50–60 minutes. Take out and discard the cinnamon stick and pour the porridge into a liquidiser. Leave to cool for 10 minutes, pour in the glucose, and liquidise until smooth. Put into a sorbetière, and churn according to the instructions with your machine. Freeze until needed. Take out of the freezer half an hour before serving.

If you don't have a sorbetière, transfer the liquidised porridge, when cold, to a plastic box. Freeze for 1 hour, by which time it should be slushy but not quite frozen, and put it back into the liquidiser. Liquidise again, and transfer it to the plastic box again and put back in the freezer. Repeat this process once more – three liquidisings and freezings altogether.

Dinner for Eight

The last menu for the autumn is for eight – again everything can be prepared in advance, even the coconut rice. This menu is equally good for parties around Christmas. All the ingredients used here will be still in good condition and easily available during the winter months.

The Menu

Hot and sour soup with prawns

◆

Roasted and grilled guineafowl
served with
Coconut rice
and
Braised red cabbage with chopped roasted peanuts and macadamia
nuts

◆

Guava and mascarpone cheese cake

ABOUT THE FOOD

Hot and sour soup with prawns

This is the best-known of all the hot and sour soups of Thailand. It is easy and quick to make, and you don't need to have it too hot or too sour either. Prepare the stock and make the soup well in advance, but put in the prawns only for 3 minutes when you are reheating the soup before serving it.

Roasted and grilled guineafowl

The guineafowl recipe is adapted from my recipe for chicken which I used to cook often at home in Indonesia, and which I still like to make in London during the summer. It is so easy to cook the birds well in advance, ready to be grilled or barbecued at any time. They will also freeze successfully – thaw them out completely before you grill them. They go very well indeed with coconut rice, as with any kind of potato dish.

Coconut rice

For those who are not accustomed to eating rice every day, plain steamed or boiled rice can taste rather bland. But coconut rice is delicious and interesting. It is quite rich and more filling than the plain boiled rice, so you will probably eat rather less of it.

Braised red cabbage with chopped roasted peanuts and macadamia nuts

I must admit that, unlike most of my other recipes, this was invented only very recently. I was considering why I had never liked red cabbage, and decided it was because it always tasted so strongly of vinegar. It was usually too sweet as well, because of the quantity of raisins or sultanas mixed with it. I like the colour, though; so I thought mixing red cabbage with crunchy nuts would taste good. And it is good – well worth the trouble of getting the macadamia nuts. But if you can't find any, the peanuts by themselves will do the job pretty well.

Guava and mascarpone cheese cake

I created this cake after making the creamed mango cake (page 100) often enough to know that it is always successful and always liked by my family and guests. The idea of using mascarpone (a creamy Italian soft cheese, available in all Italian shops) comes from my good friend Heidi Lascelles, the proprietor of the excellent 'Books for Cooks' bookshop in London. When we visited her in her beautiful house in Tuscany in the summer of 1990, she gave us a very splendid lunch of local specialities, and then produced a creamy mascarpone with apricots. This dessert was of a lovely golden colour, and the taste was subtle and cooling to the palate. The best thing is, as she told me, that it is so easy and quick to make.

For this autumn menu I chose guavas, as these are widely available now in ethnic food shops as well as in supermarkets; most of them are imported from Thailand and Brazil. I make the dish into a light cheese cake, but instead of having crumbled biscuits bound with butter as the base I use a thin layer of jelly, made from the thick guava purée and gelatine.

PLANNING AND PREPARATION

Shop early the day before the party, and spend about 90 minutes in the kitchen preparing the guineafowl and making the mascarpone cheese cake.

You need about one hour on the day of the party to finish the preparation, perhaps in the early evening, say between five and six o'clock, or earlier in the afternoon.

The day before:

Roast the guineafowl and rub them with the marinade. Keep in an ovenproof dish covered with clingfilm in the fridge.
Make the guava and mascarpone cheese cake. Store in the fridge.

On the day:

MORNING
Prepare the stock for the soup.

Prepare the prawns and the other ingredients.

Shred the red cabbage and sprinkle with salt. Leave to drain in a colander for 30 minutes.

Roast and chop the nuts. Keep in airtight containers.

Drain and rinse the cabbage to get rid of all the salt. Keep in a cool place.

Cook the rice and keep in a heatproof serving dish, covered with aluminium foil. Refrigerate.

EVENING – for 8.30 dinner

8.00   Take out everything from the fridge.
       Turn on oven to 180°C/350°F/Gas Mark 4.
       Cook the red cabbage, keep warm in the wok or pan.

8.25   Put the rice in the oven to heat.
       Assemble and finish cooking the soup.

8.30   Put the guineafowl in the oven to heat.
       SERVE THE SOUP

8.45   Take out the rice from the oven.
       Put the guineafowl under the grill.
       Heat the cabbage by stir-frying it for 2 minutes. Transfer everything to hot serving dishes.

8.50   SERVE THE MAIN COURSE

Hot and Sour Soup with Prawns

The stock for this soup should always be clear and transparent. It doesn't need to be too sour or too hot. In the original Thai version the sourness comes from tamarind, but here I use a very good chicken stock and put in the juice of one lemon just before serving.

750 g (1½ lb) uncooked large prawns, with shells

For the stock
1.5 litres (2½ pints) cold water
2–4 small dried chillies
2 kaffir lime leaves
2.5-cm (1-inch) piece of fresh ginger, peeled
5-cm (2-inch) piece of fresh or dried galingale
1 stalk fresh lemon grass, cut into three
1 medium-size onion, chopped
½ teaspoon salt
600 ml (1 pint) strong but clear chicken stock

Other ingredients
125 g (4 oz) watercress
175 g (6 oz) button mushrooms
1 tablespoon fish sauce
2 tablespoons chopped coriander leaves
juice of 1 lemon

Peel and devein the prawns. Wash the prawns, and the shells, very thoroughly. Put the prawns on a plate, sprinkle with ½ teaspoon salt and keep in the fridge until needed. Add the shells to the stock pot.

Put the water into a large saucepan with all the ingredients for the stock (except the chicken stock but including the prawn shells). Bring this to the boil and simmer for 20–30 minutes. By this time the stock will be very fragrant from the lemon grass and other aromatic ingredients. Strain the stock through a fine sieve, or a sieve lined with muslin, into another large saucepan. Discard the solids. Add the chicken stock. Keep aside to reheat later.

While the hot and sour stock is brewing, prepare the vegetables. Pick the watercress leaves off the stems as you wash them. Slice the button mushrooms finely. Put the clear, strained stock back on the stove; turn the heat up and bring the stock to a rolling boil, then add the prawns and the coriander leaves. Let the mixture boil for 2 minutes, and add the watercress and the fish sauce. Cook the soup for just *one* more minute, add the lemon juice, taste and adjust the seasoning. Divide the prawns and mushrooms equally among eight bowls, ladle the soup into the bowls, and serve hot.

Roasted and Grilled Guineafowl

Allow half a guineafowl per person. Before serving, heat the guineafowl in the oven at a high temperature for 8 minutes, then quickly put it under the grill to brown further.

4 × 1-kg (2-lb) oven-ready guineafowl
125 g (4 oz) soft butter
½ teaspoon salt

For the marinade
5 shallots, peeled and finely chopped
4 cloves garlic, peeled and finely chopped
½ teaspoon chilli powder or black pepper
2 tablespoons lemon juice
2 tablespoons light soy sauce
75 g (3 oz) finely-chopped parsley
¼ teaspoon salt
1 teaspon sugar
2 tablespoons melted butter or olive oil

Wipe the guineafowl clean, outside and inside, with kitchen paper. Rub them with the butter and salt. Roast them on a baking tray, in a preheated oven at 180°C/350°F/Gas Mark 4, for 60–70 minutes. Take them out of the oven, and let them cool.

Mix all the ingredients for the marinade in a bowl.

When the guineafowl are cool enough to touch, cut each of them in half down the back and bone them, except for the wings, thighs and drumsticks. Trim off all the fat and loosen the skin by putting your fingers underneath. Rub the marinade all over the birds, spreading it evenly under the skin as well. Choose an ovenproof dish large enough to hold the birds in a single layer. Butter the dish, and arrange them tightly with the skin side uppermost. Cover the dish with clingfilm and keep it in the fridge until needed. (Up to this point the birds can be prepared the day before.)

About 15 minutes before you are ready to serve the main course, remove the clingfilm, and put the guineafowl in the oven at 200°C/400°F/Gas Mark 6 for 8 minutes. Then grill them for a few minutes, until they are just slightly charred. Serve immediately.

Braised Red Cabbage with Chopped Roasted Peanuts and Macadamia Nuts

You can buy ready-roasted peanuts and macadamia nuts in small packets. Usually they are quite salty, so make sure that you rinse the cabbage thoroughly after leaving it mixed with salt for 30 minutes. You can of course roast your own peanuts without salt, by putting them on a baking sheet in a medium oven, shaking them from time to time, for about 15 minutes. Usually, macadamia nuts are only available already roasted and salted in supermarkets. I have seen them, around Christmas time, still in their shells; the shells are extremely hard. A good alternative is to use pecan nuts.

1 red cabbage weighing about 1.25 kg (3 lb), coarsely shredded
1–2 tablespoons salt
3 tablespoons olive oil
4 shallots, peeled and finely sliced
2 large red chillies, seeded and finely sliced
1-cm (½-inch) piece of fresh ginger, peeled and finely sliced
1 tablespoon white wine vinegar
2 tablespoons hot water
1 tablespoon light soy sauce
1 teaspoon sugar (optional)

To be added later
75 g (3 oz) roasted peanuts, roughly chopped
75 g (3 oz) roasted macadamia nuts, roughly chopped

Put the cabbage in a colander, sprinkle the salt over it, then mix salt and cabbage well with your hand. Leave it to soften for 30 minutes. Then rinse the cabbage well to get rid of all the salt.

In a wok or a large shallow saucepan, heat the oil, and fry the shallots, chillies and ginger, stirring all the time, for 3 minutes. Add the rest of the ingredients, except the cabbage, and simmer for 2 minutes. Add the cabbage, stir for a minute or so, then cover the wok or saucepan. Let it simmer for 4 minutes. Take off the cover, adjust seasoning, and continue cooking uncovered, and stirring often, for 2–3 minutes. Up to this point everything can be done in advance.

Just before serving, heat the cabbage for 2 minutes. When hot, mix in the chopped nuts, and serve immediately.

Coconut Rice

If you really don't have time to make coconut milk with desiccated coconut, which I would always suggest as the easiest way and the next best thing after freshly-grated coconut, you can use canned coconut milk. There are several brands available in ethnic shops; I recommend buying the smallest can so you won't have any left over – it spoils quite quickly once the can is open. Shake the can well before opening it. Everything you need to know about making coconut milk is on page 28.

> 500 g (1 lb) Thai fragrant or Basmati rice, soaked in cold water for at least 30 minutes but not longer than 1 hour
> 2 tablespoons clarified butter or olive oil
> ½ teaspoon salt
> 275 ml (9 fl oz) coconut milk

Drain the rice well. Heat the butter or oil in a saucepan, and when hot add the rice and the salt. Stir for a few minutes until all the rice is well coated with butter or oil. Then add the coconut milk. Stir and simmer, uncovered, until all the liquid has been absorbed. While it is simmering you need to stir the rice from time to time so that it does not stick too much to the bottom of the pan. Then take the pan off the heat and cover it tightly. Leave it undisturbed until about 20 minutes before you are ready to serve the main course.

When you are ready for the final heating, transfer the rice into an ovenproof dish. It will have become quite lumpy, so loosen it with a wooden spoon or fork as you transfer it from the pan. Cover the dish with aluminium foil, and heat in a preheated oven at 180°C/350°F/Gas Mark 4, for 20 minutes.

Guava and Mascarpone Cheese Cake

There are two kinds of guavas available in the big supermarkets: the flesh of one is light pink, the other creamy white. The outer colouring of both is between green and yellow, when they are ripe and soft inside. The flesh is full of tiny hard seeds, which are edible (though they will stick between your teeth) if you eat the guava like an apple. To make it into a purée, you need to pass it through a fine sieve before you mix it with the other ingredients.

If you don't have an Italian shop near you, and can't get mascarpone cheese, use some other kind of cream cheese; the taste will be different, but it will still be good.

You need a 20-cm (8-inch) round pie or quiche dish.

For the guava purée
2 large guavas, weighing about 150 g (5 oz) each, washed and roughly
    chopped
2 tablespoons caster sugar
1 tablespoon lemon juice
5 tablespoons cold water

For the guava jelly
15 g (½ oz) powdered gelatine
4 tablespoons caster sugar
¼ litre (8 fl oz) water
2 tablespoons lemon juice
half of the guava purée (above)

For the cheese mixture
15 g (½ oz) powdered gelatine
3 tablespoons cold water
500 g (1 lb) mascarpone cheese
the other half of the guava purée (above)
75 g (3 oz) creamy Greek yogurt

First, make the guava purée. Put the chopped guavas in a saucepan, add the rest of the ingredients for the purée, and cook on a slow heat, stirring occasionally, for 30 minutes. Transfer the mixture to a blender and blend until smooth. Then pass it through a fine sieve into a glass bowl. Divide the purée into two equal portions.

The next step is to make the jelly for the base of the cake. Put the gelatine in a small saucepan, and add 3 tablespoons of cold water. Leave aside until all the water has been absorbed. In a bigger saucepan, bring the rest of the water and the sugar to the boil. Let them bubble for 3 minutes, and stir to make sure that all the sugar has dissolved. Add one half of the guava purée, stir again, and simmer for 2 minutes. Meanwhile heat the small saucepan with the gelatine and stir until the gelatine is completely melted. Take the pan off the heat and continue stirring for a minute or so, then pour the liquid gelatine into the guava mixture. Stir again, and pour this into the dish. Cool a little, then refrigerate until set.

While the guava jelly is in the fridge, prepare the cheese mixture. Put the gelatine in a small saucepan with 3 tablespoons of cold water and leave it until the water has been absorbed or until you are ready to melt it. Put the rest of the ingredients in a blender and blend for a few seconds. Heat the saucepan with the gelatine and stir until the gelatine is completely melted. Take the pan off the heat and continue stirring for a minute or so, then pour the liquid gelatine into the cheese and guava mixture in the blender. Blend again for a few seconds. By now the guava jelly in the fridge will have set. Take it out of the fridge, and carefully pour the cheese and guava mixture on top. Level the cheese and guava with the back of a spoon, and put it back in the fridge for at least 4 hours or overnight.

To serve the cheese cake, cut it with a large knife that has been wetted with hot water, and lift each slice out of the dish with a cake slice or a spatula.

Additional Recipes

Additional Recipes

In this final section of the book I have collected a number of recipes that can be regarded as alternatives to many of those in the menus. They are traditional dishes from different countries, some of them already well-known in the West. I have adapted them, where necessary, to make them easier or quicker to prepare and cook, or to avoid the use of ingredients that are not obtainable here, but I have taken care not to lose their essential character and flavour.

Canapés and First Course Dishes

Prawn Toast

In the introduction to Yan-kit's Phoenix Rolls on page 134, I said that prawn paste is a very common ingredient all over South-East Asia, though the phoenix rolls themselves are a very sophisticated way of presenting this ingredient. The more popular way of using this prawn paste is to make this delicious snack.

Makes 24 pieces

500 g (1 lb) uncooked prawns without heads, peeled and deveined
1 teaspoon salt
1 teaspoon cornflour
¼ teaspoon sugar
1 egg white
75 g (3 oz) pork fat, minced
6 canned water chestnuts, minced
8 slices of day-old bread without crust
2 tablespoons white sesame seeds
sunflower oil for deep-frying

Put the prawns with the salt, cornflour, sugar and egg white in a blender and blend until smooth. Transfer this paste into a bowl, add the minced pork fat and water chestnuts and stir it around with a wooden spoon until everything is well mixed together. Then refrigerate for at least 30 minutes.

Cut each slice of bread into four triangles. Spread the triangles with the prawn paste, and sprinkle the sesame seeds evenly over the paste.

Half-fill a wok or a large shallow saucepan with oil, heat, and fry the triangles, pasted side down, 4 or 5 at a time, for 2 minutes. Turn them over, and as soon as the bread is golden brown remove them with a slotted spoon or a large wire scoop and drain on absorbent paper. Continue deep-frying in this way till all are done. Serve hot or warm as canapés with drinks.

Sugar Peas Rolled in Prawn Paste

This is another excellent way of using prawn paste. I find the sugar peas are a marvellous alternative to the sticks of sugar-cane the Vietnamese normally use to roll inside their prawn paste. But by all means use sugar-cane cut up into short thin sticks, if you can get it. It can occasionally be found in Indian food shops in London and elsewhere.

Makes about 50–55 prawn paste rolls

50–55 sugar peas, topped and tailed if necessary

For the prawn paste
500 g (1 lb) uncooked prawns, without heads, peeled and deveined
1 egg white
1 teaspoon salt
½ teaspoon sugar
2 teaspoons potato flour
2 cloves garlic, crushed then finely chopped
½ teaspoon finely-chopped ginger
2 teaspoons *mirin* (Japanese rice wine) (optional)

To serve the rolls
lots of crispy lettuce leaves
several small bowls of chilli fish sauce (page 197)

Put the prawns with the egg white, salt and sugar in a blender, and blend until smooth. Transfer into a glass bowl, add the flour, garlic and ginger, and stir them around with a wooden spoon until they are all well mixed together. Add the *mirin* (if used) and stir it around again for a few seconds. Refrigerate for at least 30 minutes.

Take a dessertspoonful of the prawn paste and put it on the palm of your hand. Press it flat with your other hand, and put one sugar pea in the middle, then wrap the sugar pea completely inside the paste. Make it into a nice shape by rolling it between your palms. Continue the process until all the sugar peas and the prawn paste are used up.

To cook these rolls, *either*

deep-fry them in hot oil in a wok, 7–8 rolls at a time for about 2 minutes, stirring them round all the time. Remove them with a slotted spoon or a large wire scoop to drain on a tray lined with absorbent paper.

or

arrange the rolls on a well-greased baking tray, in one layer, put the baking tray under a hot grill, and grill them for 2 minutes on one side; then turn them over and grill for another 2 minutes.

These rolls can be eaten, hot or warm, as canapés with drinks, or as a first course. The best way to serve them is with lettuce leaves (no dressing) and a bowl of fish sauce. Each person wraps a roll in a leaf and dips it into the sauce before eating it.

Sweet Potato and Prawn Cakes

Another way of using prawn paste is to make this Vietnamese prawn cake with sweet potatoes. Unlike the taro cakes in the recipe on page 159, the sweet potato here is cut into fine julienne strips or put, raw, through the rough-grating disc of your food processor. For an attractive result, save some whole prawns to decorate the cakes.

Makes 24 cakes
750 g (1½ lb) medium-size prawns (uncooked, preferably), without heads, peeled and deveined
500 g (1 lb) sweet potatoes, peeled
5 tablespoons plain flour
2 teaspoons baking powder
3 cloves garlic, finely chopped
1 teaspoon salt
a large pinch of turmeric powder
1 teaspoon sugar
½ teaspoon chilli powder
2 tablespoons finely-chopped spring onions

Set aside 24 prawns and mince the rest. Cut the sweet potatoes into fine julienne strips or grate them roughly in a food processor. Mix the sweet potatoes straight away, in a large bowl, with the remaining ingredients. Then mix in the minced prawns. Divide this mixture into 24 portions. Form each portion into a ball, with a prawn in the middle. Then with the palm of your hand press the ball slightly, to reveal a large part of the prawn. The rest of it remains well bedded into the sweet potato cake, so as not to come out when it's being fried. Continue this process until you have 24 cakes.

Deep-fry the cakes, 3 or 4 at a time, for about 1½–2 minutes each side until they are golden brown. Remove with a large slotted spoon or wire scoop, and drain on absorbent paper. Serve hot, warm or cold.

These cakes can be served as they are, as canapés with drinks, or served as a first course on some lettuce leaves with a chilli or fish sauce to dip them into.

Steamed Golden Parcels and Deep-fried Golden Parcels

Here are two more recipes using the versatile prawn paste that is so popular for snacks and small eats all over South-East Asia. For the steamed golden parcels, we use wonton skins. These can also be used for the deep-fried version, but here I make them with dried beancurd skin (see page 10).

Makes 20–24 parcels

For the wrappers
125 g (4 oz) wonton skins *or* 125 g (4 oz) dried beancurd skin, cut into
    7.5-cm (3-inch) squares; and 20–24 chives, about 10 cm (4 inches)
    long, blanched (for tying the beancurd-skin bags)

For the prawn paste
500 g (1 lb) uncooked prawns, without heads, peeled and deveined
175 g (6 oz) fillet of pork, sliced
1 egg white
1 teaspoon salt
½ teaspoon sugar
2 teaspoons cornflour or potato flour
2 cloves garlic, finely chopped
1 teaspoon finely-chopped ginger
2 teaspoons *mirin* (Japanese rice wine) (optional)

Put the prawns and slices of pork, with the egg white, salt and sugar in a blender and blend until smooth. Transfer into a glass bowl, add the flour, garlic and ginger and stir everything around with a wooden spoon until they are all mixed together. Add the *mirin* (if used) and stir it around again for a few seconds. Refrigerate for at least 30 minutes.

When you are ready to stuff the parcels, first cut off, with a pair of scissors, the four corners of the wonton skins. Put 1 teaspoonful of the filling in the centre of a wonton skin and gather the edges to make a bag. Lift this into the palm of your hand, then squeeze it gently in the middle as if to make a waist in the filled wonton. Open the bag at the top, and press the filling down with a small spoon that has been wetted with cold water, so as to make the surface of the filling flat. Repeat the process until you have 20–24 parcels. Steam the parcels in a bamboo steamer for 8–10 minutes. If you don't have a bamboo steamer, put them on an oiled plate, then put a soup plate upside down at the bottom of a large saucepan, and fill the saucepan with hot water up to the top of the plate. Then put the plate with the golden parcels on top of this. Bring the water to the boil, cover the saucepan and cook the parcels for 12–15 minutes. You might need to steam the parcels in 2 batches.

The beancurd-skin squares do not need to be trimmed off at the corners. Put a teaspoonful of the filling in the middle of a square, gather the four corners of the wrapper and tie the parcels with the chives just above the filling. Repeat the process until you have filled all the wrappers. Deep-fry these parcels, 4 or 5 at a time, for about 2 minutes. The parcels can be served hot or warm, with or without chilli sauce.

Savoury Peanut Crisps

These are definitely very superior crisps. At first glance you might think they would be tricky to make. I can assure you that this is not so, you won't need to try more than twice before you realise how easy it is. But you do need very fine rice powder, available in oriental food shops. I am afraid the rice flour or ground rice from supermarkets won't do.

Makes about 50–55 crisps
2 candlenuts
1 clove garlic
250 ml (8 fl oz) cold water
125 g (4 oz) rice powder
125 g (4 oz) raw shelled peanuts, cut in half
2 teaspoons ground coriander
1 teaspoon salt
oil for frying

Blend the candlenuts and garlic with half of the water in a blender. Transfer them to a bowl and add the rice powder. Stir with a wooden spoon until the powder is completely free of lumps, and add the rest of the ingredients. Mix well.

The crisps must be shallow-fried, then deep-fried, so you need a non-stick frying pan and a wok or a large shallow saucepan. Heat some oil in the frying pan, and half-fill the wok or saucepan with oil to deep-fry them. Take 1 tablespoon of the batter, making sure there are some peanuts in it, and pour it quickly into the frying pan. Fry it there for 1–2 minutes – you will probably be able to do 7 or 8 crisps at a time – then move the half-cooked crisps into the hot oil in the wok or saucepan. Deep-fry them for about 2 minutes until they are crisp and golden. Carry on like this until all the batter and the peanuts are used up. Drain them on a tray lined with absorbent paper. Leave them to cool before storing them. In an airtight container they will stay crisp for a fortnight or longer.

Taro Cake Stuffed with Pieces of Duck

Taro, sweet potatoes and ordinary potatoes can be used to make these little cakes or fritters, and the stuffing can be anything you fancy, minced beef, or chicken, mushrooms mixed with chicken liver, or, as here, small pieces of duck. The stuffed cakes are deep-fried until the outside is crisp. The inside is still soft, and you have another texture in the duck.

I know a lot of people who do not care for the taste of taro and sweet potato. If you are one of them, then use potato; the floury type (such as Maris Piper) are the best for this. The filling should be prepared well in advance, as it needs to be cold when you put it into the cakes.

Makes 25–28 cakes

For the filling
2 duck breasts
3 cloves garlic, finely chopped
1 teaspoon finely-chopped ginger
2 tablespoons dark soy sauce

For the taro mixture
750 g (1½ lb) taro, peeled and cut into big chunks
50 g (2 oz) lard or butter
2–3 tablespoons cornflour or potato flour
½ teaspoon salt
1 teaspoon sugar (optional)

Coat the duck breasts well with the garlic, ginger and soy sauce. Leave to stand for 30 minutes. Then either steam the duck for 1½ hours or roast in the oven at 180°C/350°F/Gas Mark 4 for 1 hour. Leave them to cool before you cut them into small pieces.

Steam or boil the taro for 25–30 minutes until they are well cooked. If you boil them, drain the water off as soon as the taro are cooked. Put the taro in a large bowl and mash them until smooth. When they are cool enough to touch, add the rest of the ingredients and knead for a few minutes. Then divide the mixture into 25 or 28 small balls.

To fill each cake: put a taro ball on a well-floured flat surface, flatten it with a small rolling pin, and put a piece of duck in the middle. Close it up to make a sort of little semi-circular pasty. Pinch the edges to seal it. Continue filling the taro cakes until all the mixture and the filling have been used up. Deep-fry the cakes, 4 or 5 at a time, for 1–1½ minutes each side, or until they are golden brown and crisp. Take them out with a large slotted spoon or wire scoop and drain them on a tray lined with absorbent paper. Serve hot, warm or cold.

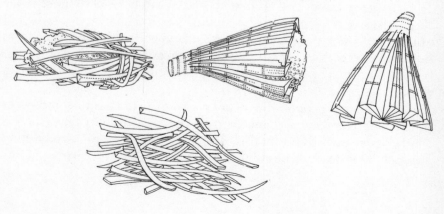

Lentil Fritters

These fritters are normally eaten with Burmese fish soup (page 169), but they are also very good by themselves as snacks at any time of the day.

Makes 30–32 fritters

2 tablespoons sesame or groundnut oil
1 onion, finely chopped
1 teaspoon ground coriander
1 teaspoon salt
250 g (8 oz) red or green lentils, soaked in water for 1 hour, then drained
150 ml (¼ pint) cold water

To be added later
4 tablespoons chopped spring onions or Chinese chives
5 tablespoons plain flour or rice powder
1 tablespoon cornflour
1 egg, beaten
¼ teaspoon ground white pepper
200 ml (7 fl oz) vegetable oil for frying

Heat the sesame or groundnut oil in a wok or frying pan and fry the onion for 2 minutes, then add the ground coriander, salt and lentils. Stir-fry these for 2 minutes, then add the water. Simmer, stirring often, for 5 minutes or until all the water has been absorbed by the lentils. Leave to cool.

When cool add the rest of the ingredients. Mix well and adjust seasoning. Heat the oil for frying in a frying pan, and drop in the batter, a heaped teaspoonful at a time. Fry about 7 or 8 spoonfuls in one go, for 1–1½ minutes each side, turning them over once. Take them out with a slotted spoon and drain on absorbent paper. Serve hot, warm or cold as an accompaniment to *Mohinga* (page 169), or as a snack.

Stuffed Bamboo Shoots

This is a Laotian recipe I adapted from Phia Sing's *Traditional Recipes of Laos*, published by Prospect Books.

Although the young bamboo shoot tips (available in cans in oriental grocers) are recommended for this recipe, the standard-sized canned bamboo shoots, more widely available, are also suitable. In both cases you need a small, very sharp knife to shred the bamboo shoots into fine julienne strips. If using the young tips, start each cut about 1 cm (½ inch) below the tip of the shoot, so you have an umbrella-like shape and can push some of the stuffing into the middle. If using the more mature bamboo shoots, lay some of the julienne strips on a flat surface, put a rounded teaspoonful of the stuffing onto them, then lay more bamboo strips on top. Roll these into a cylinder or cone – the stuffing will hold it together. Repeat the process until all the bamboo shoots and the stuffing are used up.

Serves 4–6 as a starter or accompaniment to the main course

500 g (1 lb) canned bamboo shoots, drained, rinsed thoroughly under the
    cold tap, and cut into fine julienne strips

For the stuffing
175 g (6 oz) tenderloin of pork, minced
6–7 shallots (125–150 g/4–5 oz), very finely chopped
4 tablespoons finely-chopped spring onions
1 teaspoon fish sauce
a pinch of salt
½ teaspoon freshly-ground black pepper
1 tablespoon plain flour

Other ingredients
2 eggs
1 tablespoon plain flour
a pinch of salt
groundnut oil for deep-frying

Mix all the ingredients for the stuffing in a bowl. Form a small ball about the size of a walnut from this mixture, fry or grill it, and taste for seasoning. Carefully add more salt or fish sauce if needed. (Remember that the fish sauce is very salty indeed.)

Stuff the bamboo shoots (see the introduction above). Arrange the stuffed shoots in a single layer on a baking sheet. Then put them under the grill, and grill them for 4 minutes. Alternatively, cover the bamboo shoots with aluminium foil and bake in the oven at 180°C/350°F/Gas Mark 4 for 10 minutes. Leave to cool.

Mix and beat the eggs with the flour and a pinch of salt. Heat some oil in a deep-fryer or wok. Dip each stuffed bamboo shoot in the beaten egg and fry in the hot oil, a few at a time, for 3–4 minutes or until golden brown. Take them out with a slotted spoon and drain them on absorbent paper. Serve as a starter, hot, warm or cold, with some lettuce leaves and chilli sauce. They can also be served with the main course.

Golden Cups

These may be time-consuming to make, but they are among those small eats that never fail to attract praise and compliments. They can be filled with an endless variety of fillings, vegetable, meat or fish. The cups originated as banana-leaf cups or baskets, filled with food as offerings to Hindu gods in the temples of Bali. In Thailand, similar banana-leaf cups, called *krathong*, are floated on rivers and ponds during the Buddhist water festival in November. Anyway, you can make hundreds of these golden cups in an hour or two, very cheaply, so they are very suitable for a large cocktail party. Fill the cups just before serving.

As with all the rice-flour recipes in this book, you should use the very finest rice powder available in most ethnic shops. For the filling, I give a choice here between a pork filling from North Thailand and an aubergine filling from Indonesia. The fillings can be made well in advance and refrigerated for up to 24 hours. Leave them out of the fridge to get them back to room temperature before serving.

The scoop or mould to make the cups is available from large Thai shops, with either two or four cup-moulds on one handle (picture on page 176).

Makes 150–160 cups

For the cups
75 g (3 oz) plain flour
75 g (3 oz) rice powder
400 ml (14 fl oz) cold water
a tiny pinch of salt
vegetable oil for deep-frying

Put the flour in a bowl, add the rest of the ingredients and mix them well with a wooden spoon until you get a smooth batter.

The best way to cook golden cups is to use a deep-fryer with a thermostat, because you need to keep the oil temperature between 180° and 200°C (350° and 400°F). But you can use a wok if you don't mind turning the gas up and down while frying to regulate the temperature of the oil. Heat the oil to the required temperature and put the mould in the oil, initially for 4 minutes to get it really hot. Dip the outside of the hot mould up to the brim in the batter and leave it there for 8–10 seconds. Don't let any batter overflow into the mould. A layer of the batter will start to cook and will adhere to the bottom of the mould. Now plunge the mould into the hot oil. Hold it there for 10 seconds before shaking the batter 'cups' off the scoop and into the oil. (You may need to give them a push with a fork or chopsticks to free them.) Let them deep-fry a few more seconds till they really are golden, then remove with a slotted spoon or chopsticks and let them drain on a tray lined with absorbent paper. Continue as before until all the batter has been used up. When cool, store them in an airtight container for later use. They will keep crisp for about a week provided the container is really airtight.

For the pork filling
3 tablespoons groundnut oil
4 cloves garlic, finely chopped
4 large red chillies, seeded and finely chopped
500 g (1 lb) fillet of pork, minced
2 teaspoons finely-chopped coriander leaves
2 teaspoons whole green or black peppercorns, coarsely ground
3 kaffir lime leaves, finely shredded
2 teaspoons finely-chopped basil leaves
1 teaspoon sugar
2 tablespoons fish sauce or light soy sauce

Heat the oil in a wok or frying pan, and fry the garlic and chillies, stirring all the time, for 1 minute, then add the minced pork. Stir-fry for 2–3 minutes, then add the rest of the ingredients, and continue stir-frying for 2–3 more minutes or until the meat is almost dry. Adjust the seasoning, and leave to cool to room temperature before filling the cups just before they are to be served.

For the aubergine filling

3 medium-size aubergines, roasted whole in the oven on 180°C/350°F/Gas
    Mark 4 for 30–35 minutes
3 tablespoons groundnut or olive oil
2 small onions, finely chopped
2 cloves garlic, finely chopped
2 green chillies, seeded and finely chopped
2 teaspoons ground coriander
3 tablespoons finely-chopped mint or parsley
1 teaspoon salt

When the aubergines are cool, cut them in halves lengthways, and scoop out the flesh with a spoon. Chop the flesh finely.

Heat the oil in a wok or frying pan, and fry the onion, garlic and chillies for 2 minutes, stirring all the time. Add the rest of the ingredients, except the mint or parsley. Stir and adjust seasoning. Stir in the mint or parsley and transfer the aubergine mixture to an ovenproof dish. Cover the dish and bake in the oven at 180°C/350°F/Gas Mark 4 for 20–25 minutes. Leave the mixture to cool to room temperature before filling the cups with it.

Any leftovers from the filling can be served on top of crisp lettuce or chicory.

Miniature Spring Rolls

Miniature spring rolls are normally served as a starter in Thai restaurants. I have served them many times as finger food at drinks parties, and as a first course. You can vary the filling, using prawns with pork, chicken or crab meat, or you can have a vegetable filling. Here is one with prawn and pork.

The wrappers can be bought in oriental supermarkets, usually from the freezer (see page 20).

Makes about 50 rolls

1 packet of 50 spring roll wrappers, 12.5 cm (5 inches) square

For the filling
100 g (3½ oz) packet cellophane noodles
250 g (8 oz) uncooked prawns without shells
125 g (4 oz) pork with some fat, minced
4 carrots, peeled and cut into tiny matchsticks
125 g (4 oz) white cabbage, finely shredded
15 g (½ oz) woodears fungus, soaked in hot water for 4 minutes, rinsed
    and chopped
5 spring onions, cut into small rounds
2 cloves of garlic, crushed
½ teaspoon finely-chopped ginger
½ teaspoon chilli powder
1 teaspoon salt
1 tablespoon light soy sauce
1 egg
vegetable oil for frying

To serve
crisp lettuce leaves
mint and/or coriander leaves
chilli fish sauce (page 197)

Assuming the wrappers are bought frozen, thaw them out completely and carefully peel each one from the pile. Then cover them with a tea towel to prevent them from drying.

Soak the cellophane noodles in hot water for 3 minutes, drain and cut up roughly. In a large bowl mix all the ingredients except the egg and the oil. Separate the egg, mix the yolk thoroughly into the filling, and save the white in a bowl (you will need it for sealing the rolls).

Put a wrapper on a flat surface (e.g. a plate or tray); put about 2 teaspoons of the filling onto the corner nearest you. Pull the corner over the filling and roll up the wrapper with the filling inside it, but leave the corner furthest from you free, like the flap of an envelope. Then fold the two side flaps towards the centre, brush the remaining flap with egg white and fold it so that the roll is sealed. Repeat the process until all the rolls are made and sealed. Deep-fry the rolls, 6 or 8 at a time, in hot oil until golden brown and crisp. Serve hot. The way to eat spring rolls is to wrap each one in a lettuce leaf, put in a leaf or two of mint or coriander, then dip it into the sauce.

Fish Boats

These are delicious canapés to serve with pre-dinner drinks or at a drinks party. They are little boat-shaped red and yellow sweet peppers filled with chopped white fish or canned tuna fish mixed with some aromatic Asian herbs and spices.

Makes 24–32 fish boats

2 red and 2 yellow peppers, seeded
2 shallots, chopped
2 cloves garlic, chopped
3 candlenuts or macadamia nuts or blanched almonds
2 tablespoons groundnut or olive oil
2 tablespoons cold water
1 teaspoon ground coriander
½ teaspoon ground cumin
1 teaspoon chilli powder
125 ml (4 fl oz) water
2 tablespoons desiccated coconut (optional)
225–340 g (8–12 oz) boneless whitefish steaks, chopped, or 2 × 170-g
  (6-oz) cans tuna fish, drained and flaked
2 tablespoons chopped coriander leaves
2 tablespoons chopped mint
1 tablespoon lime juice
salt to taste

Cut the peppers into 6–8 little wedges, wash, and wipe dry with kitchen paper.

Put the shallots, garlic and nuts with the oil and 2 tablespoons of water in a blender. Blend until smooth, then transfer into a small saucepan. Add the ground coriander, cumin and chilli powder, and the 125 ml (4 fl oz) of water. Stir and bring this mixture to the boil, stir again, turn down the flame, add the desiccated coconut (if used) and let it simmer for 6 minutes, stirring occasionally. Add the fish, stir and cook for 3 minutes. Put in the rest of the ingredients and salt to taste. Stir again, and when there is no more sauce or surplus liquid, but the fish mixture is still moist, take the pan off the stove. Cool to room temperature and divide the filling among the sweet-pepper boats. Arrange them on a platter, cover with clingfilm and refrigerate until needed.

Stuffed Javanese Rice Cakes

These Javanese rice cakes are made with glutinous rice and stuffed with slightly spiced shredded chicken meat. They are among the most popular street foods, and as they are wrapped in banana leaves they are not exposed to hungry flies or street dust. Here I make them in a Swiss roll tin, cutting them up just like a Swiss roll.

Use the same cup to measure the rice and the coconut milk. You'll need a 22.5 × 32.5 cm (9 × 13 inch) Swiss roll tin and some grease-proof paper.

Makes 10–12 slices

2 cups glutinous rice, soaked in cold water for 40–60 minutes, then
    drained
2 cups coconut milk (page 27)
¼ teaspoon salt

For the stuffing
2 chicken breasts
4 shallots, chopped
3 cloves garlic, chopped
3 candlenuts or macadamia nuts or blanched almonds
1 teaspoon ground coriander
½ teaspoon ground cumin
½ teaspoon brown sugar
1 kaffir lime leaf (optional)
½ teaspoon salt
¼ teaspoon ground white pepper
2 tablespoons groundnut or olive oil
150 ml (¼ pint) thick coconut milk

Boil the glutinous rice in the coconut with ¼ teaspoon salt until all the liquid has been absorbed by the rice. Then transfer this rice into a steamer or a double saucepan, and steam it for 15 minutes. Turn off the heat, but leave the rice in the steamer until you are ready with the stuffing.

Boil the chicken breasts with water and a large pinch of salt for about 40 minutes. Take them out of the stock, and leave to cool on a plate. When cool shred them finely.

Put the rest of the ingredients for the stuffing with only half of the coconut milk into a blender and blend until smooth. Transfer this thick liquid into a small saucepan. Bring to the boil and simmer for 8 minutes. Add the shredded chicken meat and the rest of the coconut milk and continue to simmer until all the coconut milk has been absorbed by the meat, but the mixture is still moist. Adjust the seasoning, and leave to cool.

Line the Swiss roll tin with a sheet of greaseproof paper and spread the rice on this, pressing it down with another piece of greaseproof paper to fill the tin evenly. Now spread the cool spiced chicken evenly on top of the rice. Then roll this as if you were making a Swiss roll. Cut it into slices with a large knife that has been wetted with hot water. Serve warm or cold as a tea-time snack, or with drinks in the evening.

Burmese Fish Soup

This is the national dish of Burma, and is called *Mohinga*. Like the rice vermicelli soup in the Summer Menu (pages 111, 114) which originated in Malaysia, this Burmese soup can be served as a party dish or a one-dish meal, with all the accompanying ingredients spread on a large plate and the soup in a bowl next to it, kept piping hot on the hotplate. The guests can help themselves to what they like. One ingredient traditionally used in *Mohinga*, which at the time of writing is still not available in the West, is banana trunk. However, this can be easily and suitably replaced with fresh banana flowers (available in oriental shops in large cities), or canned heart of palm, which is usually available in good delicatessens. The Burmese also use powdered roasted rice to thicken the soup a little but I find this is quite unnecessary, as the rice noodles will soak up the runny soup very well.

After trying this soup with different kinds of white fish, I decided the best fish to use here are conger eels and monkfish. You need to be diligent in extracting bones from the conger eel, but monkfish is a beautiful fish for *Mohinga*. Assuming you buy only the tail end, not the whole fish, the flesh can be easily filleted and the thick bones go to the stock pot.

Serves 6–8, or more for a buffet party

500 g (1 lb) monkfish tails

For the fish stock
750 g (1½ lb) conger eel
the bones of the monkfish tails
1.5 litres (2½ pints) water
3 fresh or dried red chillies, cut in halves
¼ teaspoon ground turmeric
2 stalks lemon grass
1 tablespoon fish sauce

First, fillet the monkfish tails so that you can put the bones into the stock pot. Put all the ingredients for the stock in a large saucepan and bring to the boil. Simmer for 5 minutes, then take out the conger eel, and leave it to cool on a plate while the stock pot is still simmering. When the eel is cool enough to handle, separate the flesh from the skin and bones. Reserve the flesh and put the skin and bones back into the pot. Continue to simmer this for 30 more minutes, then strain the stock into a bowl. Discard the solids. Meanwhile prepare the rest of the ingredients.

For the accompaniments
1 banana flower, 2 layers of the outer leaves discarded, or 500 g (1 lb)
    canned heart of palm, cut into 1 cm (½ inch)-thick rounds
500 g (1 lb) rice stick noodles or rice vermicelli
some basic chilli sauce for the soup (page 193)
fried onion flakes (see page 197)
4 hard-boiled duck or hen eggs, peeled and quartered, or 12 quail eggs
lentil fritters (page 161)
2–3 tablespoons chopped flat-leaf parsley

If using banana flower, boil this whole in slightly-salted water for 6–8 minutes. Drain and quarter it, then cut the quartered flower into thickish slices. If using hearts of palm, drain and rinse them before cutting. Put these to one side on a large serving dish. Boil the noodles for 2–3 minutes, drain them, and put them next to the banana flower slices or hearts of palm. Arrange the rest of the accompaniments on the same dish, with the chilli sauce in a small bowl in the centre. Keep these aside, they don't need to be served very hot as long as the soup is piping hot.

To finish the fish soup
2 tablespoons groundnut oil
3 shallots, finely sliced
3 cloves garlic, finely sliced
1 large red chilli, seeded and finely sliced
1 teaspoon finely-chopped ginger
5-cm (2½-inch) piece of lemon grass, outer leaves discarded, the soft
    inner part finely chopped
900 ml (1½ pints) thick coconut milk (page 27)
the boneless flesh from the conger eel
the monkfish fillets, cut into bite-sized pieces
salt and pepper to taste

Heat the oil in a largish saucepan and fry all the sliced and chopped
ingredients, stirring continuously, for 2 minutes. Add the coconut
milk, bring to the boil and add the fish. Simmer for 4 minutes, then add
some of the strained fish stock. Use your own judgement here as to how
much you need in order to serve 6 or 8 people, or more. Adjust the
seasoning.

To serve, put the noodles and some of the other accompaniments
into individual soup bowls, then ladle the hot fish soup into them. The
lentil fritters can be eaten separately, as you would eat bread or rolls
when serving soup western style.

Red Lentil Soup

Another Burmese recipe, but this one is a very simple everyday soup.
The fried onion flakes used here, and in some other soups in this book,
can be bought from many supermarkets and oriental food shops.

Serves 4

250 g (8 oz) dried red lentils
1 red or green chilli, seeded and finely chopped (optional)
1 teaspoon finely-chopped ginger
3 cloves garlic, finely chopped
5-cm (2½-inch) piece of lemon grass, outer leaves discarded, and the
    inner soft part finely chopped
3 tablespoons sesame or olive oil
1.2 litres (2 pints) water
salt and pepper to taste
some fried onion flakes to garnish

Wash and soak the lentils for one hour. Then drain. Fry the chilli (if used), ginger, garlic and lemon grass in the sesame or olive oil, stirring all the time, for 1 minute, then add the lentils. Cook on a moderate heat, stirring from time to time, for about 5 minutes or until the mixture becomes slightly brown. Add the water, and cook until the soup is quite thick, about 8–10 minutes. Adjust the seasoning. Put the fried onion flakes into the soup bowls just before serving the soup hot.

Grilled Lobster with Piquant Thai Sauce

It goes almost without saying that the best lobster to use is a live one. Failing that, cooked lobster from a good fishmonger will still be very good and will also shorten the preparation and cooking time. Ask your fishmonger to cut the cooked lobster in half lengthways and to discard all the inedible parts of the lobster for you; they are the head sac, the gills (which look like fingers) and the intestinal vein (some fishmongers sell lobsters already 'dressed'). When you get home, you have only to take out the meat from the claws. Crack each claw with the back of a knife in two places, without crushing the meat. Break up the pincers and pull them away from the meat. Pull the meat out and pile it on the head shell.

If you can get a live lobster, plunge it in boiling water for about 4–5 minutes until the colour turns red. Then halve, clean and prepare it as above. You can sometimes buy a frozen whole lobster; in this case I recommend buying an uncooked one. Thaw it out completely before boiling it.

Serves 2

1 large cooked lobster or 2 smaller ones, cut in half lengthways
2 tablespoons soft butter

For the sauce
2 small red chillies, seeded and finely chopped
1 tablespoon chopped Chinese chives, or spring onions
1 tablespoon chopped coriander leaves
1 teaspoon grated ginger
1 clove garlic, crushed
2 tablespoons fish sauce (*nam pla*)
1 tablespoon mild vinegar or lemon juice
1 teaspoon sugar (optional)

Mix all the ingredients for the sauce in a small glass bowl. Keep in a cool place until needed.

Just before grilling the lobster, spread the soft butter on the lobster meat. Arrange the lobster halves side by side on a heatproof dish or a baking tray, and put the dish or tray under a hot grill. Grill for 3 minutes, then spread the sauce in equal quantities over the lobster halves. You can put them under the grill for 1 more minute, if you wish. Serve hot.

Grapefruit Salad with Salmon and Monkfish

This salad is easy to make and looks very attractive as one of the dishes for a buffet party, or served immediately as the first course of a dinner party.

Serves 4–6 as a first course

For the grapefruit salad
1 pink grapefruit, segmented
1 green grapefruit, segmented
mixed varieties of lettuce leaves, including radicchio, roughly shredded
10–12 coriander or mint leaves
1 tablespoon lime or lemon juice

For the fish
2 tablespoons olive oil
1 small onion, finely sliced
2 cloves garlic, crushed
2 small red chillies, seeded and finely chopped, or a large pinch of chilli powder
5-cm (2-inch) piece of lemon grass, outer leaves discarded, finely chopped
1 teaspoon finely-chopped ginger
2 tablespoons fish sauce or light soy sauce
2 tablespoons rice or white wine vinegar
8 tablespoons hot water
2 teaspoons hot mustard (optional)
375 g (12 oz) salmon fillet, cut into bite-sized pieces
375 g (12 oz) monkfish fillet, cut into bite-sized pieces

Put the grapefruit segments in a bowl. Use the lettuce and coriander or mint leaves to line a serving dish, and sprinkle them with the lime/lemon juice.

Heat the oil in a large frying pan and fry all the chopped and sliced ingredients, stirring all the time, for 2 minutes. Add the fish or soy sauce and vinegar, water and mustard (if used), and simmer for about 2 minutes. Then add the fish pieces. Simmer for another 3 minutes. Take off the heat and let the fish cool to room temperature. When cool, arrange the grapefruit segments on top of the lettuce leaves and the fish on top of the grapefruit. Pour the cooking juices over the salad. Chill for 30 minutes or longer, and serve.

Prawn Salad

A variation of the grapefruit and fish salad, which can be served as a light lunch or first course, accompanied by slices of brown bread and butter or by hot garlic bread.

Serves 4 as a light lunch dish or 6 as a first course

1 kg (2 lb) uncooked king prawns, peeled
½ teaspoon salt
8 tablespoons groundnut oil for frying

For the dressing
2 small red chillies, seeded and finely chopped
5-cm (2-inch) piece of lemon grass, outer leaves discarded, then finely chopped
2 fresh kaffir lime leaves, finely shredded
2 tablespoons fish sauce or light soy sauce
2 tablespoons lemon juice
1 tablespoon mild vinegar
1 teaspoon caster sugar

For the garnish
10 picked mint leaves
10 picked coriander leaves
a small radicchio, cut into four, then the leaves loosened and wiped clean with kitchen paper

Cut each peeled prawn down the back into two halves, removing and discarding the black vein at the same time. Wash the prawns under a cold tap, drain them in a colander and pat them dry with kitchen paper. Transfer into a glass bowl and mix in the ½ teaspoon of salt. Keep in a cool place or in the fridge.

Mix all the ingredients for the dressing in a glass bowl.

Heat the oil in a wok or a small but deep frying pan. When hot fry the prawns in three batches for 2–3 minutes each batch. Drain in a colander.

Put the prawns into a bowl with the dressing, and mix them well. Leave them to cool, then chill them for 30 minutes.

Before serving, mix in all the garnish.

Coconut Prawn on Omelette Nets

The Thai marinade for these prawns is so good that it is a pity to throw it away. I suggest you stir 2 tablespoons of rice or plain flour into it, and use it as a batter for frying the prawns. Or if, like me, you prefer your prawns fried without batter, use it to fry some vegetables, such as cauliflower florets or small button mushrooms, and serve the vegetables on a side dish to be eaten together with the prawns or with the main course.

Serves 6 as a first course

For the omelette nets
4 large eggs and 1 egg white
vegetable oil

Make the omelette nets well in advance and stack them on a plate, separated from each other by pieces of greaseproof paper. Serve them cold to line the plates you are going to serve the prawns on.

To make the nets: break the eggs into a bowl, add the extra egg white, and with a fork break the yolks. Do not beat, but just gently mix the yolks and the whites with the fork. Oil a round non-stick frying pan, heat it, and start making the nets. Hold a strainer – a conical one is best – over the hot pan, and pour some of the egg into it. Move the strainer so that the egg that streams out makes a net pattern in the pan. Rest the sieve on a bowl or jug, by which time the net will be cooked. Transfer the omelette net to a plate. Continue making nets until you have used all the egg; make sure you have at least six.

For the prawns

24–30 king prawns, peeled, with the tails left on, the body then split into
   two but the two halves still joined at the tail
150 ml (¾ pint) groundnut or sunflower oil for frying

For the marinade

100 g (4 oz) creamed coconut, roughly chopped
250 ml (8 fl oz) hot water
2.5-cm (1-inch) piece of fresh galingale, chopped, or ½ teaspoon
   galingale powder (page 13)
5-cm (2-inch) piece of lemon grass, outer leaves discarded, chopped
2 kaffir leaves, washed and chopped
3 shallots, chopped
2 cloves garlic, chopped
2 small fresh or dried chillies, or a large pinch of coarsely-ground white
   pepper
1 tablespoon lemon juice
1 teaspoon salt

Put all the ingredients for the marinade in a blender or food processor
and blend them until smooth. Transfer them to a glass bowl and mix in
the prawns. Keep refrigerated for at least 2 hours.

When ready to fry, drain the excess marinade from the prawns by
putting them in a colander. (Save the marinade if you wish to make a
batter to fry some vegetables, as explained in the introduction above.)
Heat the oil in a wok or deep-fryer, and fry the prawns in two or three
batches, each batch for 2 minutes only.

To serve: line six plates with an omelette net each and arrange the
prawns on top. Serve immediately.

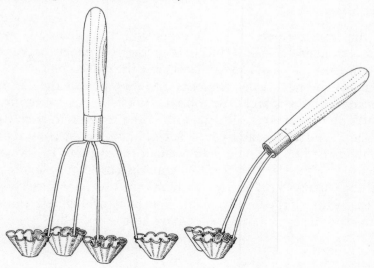

Main Course Dishes

Burmese Chicken Curry with Lime

Whether authentic or not, this Burmese curry is extraordinarily good. It has chopped tomatoes among the ingredients, which made me a little doubtful at first, because a long time ago a Burmese friend of mine who is an excellent cook told me (in Indonesia) that you just don't put tomatoes in curry. But this recipe was given to me by another friend, here in London, whose mother is Burmese, and who is also an extremely good cook.

The *balachaung* (a chilli-hot Burmese relish made of prawns or shrimps) which is used here is a home-made prawn *balachaung* (page 192), but you can buy ready-made and preserved *balachaung* in jars from oriental food shops.

Serves 4

3 tablespoons sesame or groundnut oil
2 medium onions, finely chopped
3 cloves garlic, finely chopped
1 teaspoon ground turmeric
1 tablespoon ground coriander
3 cinnamon sticks
6 cloves
2 kaffir lime leaves
1 stalk lemon grass, cut into two and bruised
4 chicken breasts or 8 chicken thighs, boned
1 can chopped tomatoes
juice of 3 limes
3 tablespoons *balachaung* (see page 192)
1 teaspoon freshly-ground black pepper
1 tablespoon fish sauce
some hot water, if necessary
some salt, if necessary

Heat the oil in a large saucepan and fry the onions and garlic for 1–2 minutes, stirring all the time. Add the turmeric, ground coriander, cinnamon sticks, cloves, kaffir lime leaves and lemon grass, and stir again for 1 minute. Add the chicken pieces, stir these around and cook on a medium heat until they are brown. Add the rest of the ingredients except hot water and salt, cover the pan and simmer for 10 minutes. Uncover the pan, stir the whole thing, add some water if necessary, and continue cooking, uncovered this time, for another 10–12 minutes or until the chicken is tender. Remove the chicken to a hot serving dish, and keep it warm in the oven while you continue cooking the sauce in the saucepan until it is thick and oily. Adjust the seasoning and spoon out some of the oil, then pour the sauce onto the chicken. Serve hot immediately with lots of plain cooked rice.

Baked and Grilled Chicken, Menado-style

Allow half a small chicken per person for this traditionally very hot dish. You can use something like 20–30 large red chillies for this, but here I suggest using red tomatoes with just a few chillies. It will taste better and be kinder to your palate and stomach.

Serves 4

2 small chickens, weighing about 1.1 kg (2½ lb) each
juice of 1 lime or lemon
1 teaspoon salt
2 tablespoons groundnut or olive oil

For the paste
8 shallots or 2 small onions, chopped
3 cloves garlic, chopped
3 large red chillies, seeded and chopped
1 teaspoon finely-chopped ginger
1 teaspoon shrimp or anchovy paste
2 tablespoons groundnut oil
2 tablespoons water
6 red tomatoes, peeled, seeded and chopped
salt to taste

Split the chickens lengthways into halves and trim off some of the skin, fat and bones. Wipe the chickens inside and out with a damp tea towel. Then rub the chickens with the lime or lemon juice, salt and oil. Leave in a cool place.

Put all the ingredients for the paste, except the tomatoes and salt, in a blender and blend until smooth. Put the paste in a small saucepan, bring this to the boil and stir continuously for 4 minutes. Add the chopped tomatoes and continue cooking and stirring for a minute or so. Adjust the seasoning and remove from the stove to cool to room temperature.

When the paste is cool, use half of it to rub the chicken halves, rubbing under the skin as well. Then put the chicken halves on a large piece of aluminium foil, side by side. Spread the rest of the tomato and chilli paste on top of all the chicken halves equally. Fold the foil over the top to make a parcel, and fold the edges over to seal it roughly.

Bake in the oven at 180°C/350°F/Gas Mark 4 for 50–60 minutes. Transfer the chickens to a heatproof serving dish and put this under the grill for 3–4 minutes, or until the top surfaces of the chickens are quite charred. Serve immediately, with rice, potatoes or pasta.

Korean Beef and Mushroom Casserole

This Korean casserole is very easy to prepare and cook, and ideal for a meal for two. But there is no reason not to make it for more people. I have adapted the ingredients to what is available in the West.

Serves 2

125 g (4 oz) fresh shiitake mushrooms, stalks removed, and sliced
3 tablespoons sesame oil
¼ teaspoon salt
200 g (7 oz) fillet or rump steak, sliced into very thin strips
1 onion, very finely sliced
1 small bunch watercress, trimmed and cleaned
2 pak choy or 6 leaves of Chinese cabbage, roughly shredded
2 medium-size carrots, peeled and sliced very thin diagonally

For the spice mixture
2 tablespoons light soy sauce
2 teaspoons sugar
3 cloves garlic, crushed in a garlic crusher
1 tablespoon roasted sesame seeds, pounded in a mortar with a pestle
2 tablespoons finely-chopped spring onions

To be added later
1 tablespoon light soy sauce
¼ teaspoon salt and pepper mixture
250 ml (8 fl oz) hot water

Put the sliced mushrooms in a bowl and mix in 1 tablespoonful of the sesame oil and the salt. Keep aside.

In another bowl mix all the spice mixture ingredients, and marinade the slices of beef for at least 30 minutes.

Heat the remaining 2 tablespoons of sesame oil in a casserole – a round one, if possible – and stir-fry the beef for 2–3 minutes. Turn down the heat, and arrange the beef in a pile to one side of the casserole, filling one segment of the circle. Then place the other ingredients, except the mushrooms, clockwise in small heaps to fill the remaining segments of the casserole, leaving an empty space in the centre. Pile the mushrooms in this central space.

Stir the soy sauce and salt and pepper into the hot water, and pour this over the vegetables in the casserole. Cover it, and simmer for 6–8 minutes. Serve hot with rice.

Chilli Beef with Fried Basil

This dish is only for those who like the hot taste of chilli, and can eat plenty of rice. The rice will absorb the hotness of the chilli, then you will realise how good the beef and the basil are.

Serves 2

300 g (10 oz) rump steak, cut into thin strips

For the marinade
2–3 large red chillies, seeded and chopped
4 cloves garlic, chopped
1 teaspoon chopped ginger
2 tablespoons fish sauce
1 teaspoon sugar
2 tablespoons lemon juice
1 tablespoon chopped basil

150 ml (¼ pint) groundnut oil
18–20 basil leaves, wiped dry
salt to taste
2 tablespoons *mirin* (Japanese rice wine) or dry white wine

Put all the ingredients for the marinade except the chopped basil into a blender and blend until smooth. Transfer this to a bowl, mix in the chopped basil and marinate the beef for at least 30 minutes.

Heat the groundnut oil in a wok or frying pan and fry the basil leaves for 1–2 minutes until they become transparent. Leave to cool. When cold the fried basil will be crisp.

Discard most of the oil except about 2–3 tablespoonsful. Heat it again and add the beef. Stir-fry for 3–4 minutes on a high heat, splash in the *mirin*, stir and adjust the seasoning, then add the crispy basil. Serve straight away with plenty of rice.

Fried Duck with Five Flavours

The five flavours here are not exactly the Chinese five spices, but a Thai combination of five fragrant spices and herbs. Here I use duck breasts, marinated, then steamed and deep-fried until the skins are crisp.

Serves 4

4 Aylesbury duck breasts

For the marinade
3 kaffir lime leaves, shredded
the inner part of 1 stem of lemon grass, chopped
½ teaspoon ground cinnamon
1 teaspoon ground coriander
1 teaspoon chopped ginger
2 tablespoons dark soy sauce
2 tablespoons fish sauce or light soy sauce
2 tablespoons water

vegetable oil for deep-frying

Put all the ingredients for the marinade in a blender, and blend until smooth. Transfer into a bowl and marinate the duck breasts for at least 2 hours or overnight in the fridge. Turn the duck breasts several times during this time.

Steam the duck for 1¼–1½ hours. Then deep-fry in hot oil for 4–5 minutes or until the skins are crisp. Serve hot with fried rice and salad or some cooked vegetables.

Duck with Exotic Stuffing

This is no harder to prepare than any other stuffed poultry. What makes this recipe particularly delicious is the fresh shiitake mushrooms, which are available from large supermarkets, and the coconut milk, which you make from creamed coconut diluted in hot water. For 6 tablespoonsful of coconut milk, grate or chop 60–90 g (2–3 oz) of creamed coconut, and dilute with 5 tablespoonsful of hot water. If you really can't get creamed coconut, substitute single cream for it. To steam the duck, which will make it lovely and juicy, you need a large steamer or double saucepan, or, failing this, a large saucepan or even a wok with a domed lid. The stuffed duck needs to be placed on a plate or bowl so that you can save the juice for the sauce.

Sweet rice is flattened green rice, usually imported from Thailand. If you cannot obtain it, use rice flakes (available from supermarkets) or fresh breadcrumbs.

To serve 4–6

2 kg (4½ lb) oven-ready Aylesbury duck, rubbed inside and out with
   1 teaspoon salt

For the stuffing
2–3 red chillies, seeded
4 shallots, peeled
2 cloves garlic
6 tablespoons thick coconut milk (see introduction above)
the duck liver, chopped (optional)
250 g (8 oz) fresh shiitake mushrooms, thinly sliced
125 g (4 oz) pork tenderloin, minced
2 tablespoons chopped coriander leaves
2 tablespoons finely-chopped spring onions
1 tablespoon fish sauce (*nam pla*)
½ teaspoon salt
¾ teaspoon ground white pepper
3 tablespoons sweet rice

Blend the chillies, shallots, garlic and coconut milk together until smooth. Mix with the other stuffing ingredients in a bowl. You need to fry a small ball of this stuffing to taste the seasoning. Add more salt if necessary, and stuff the mixture into the body cavity of the duck. Sew up the skin, or pin it together with wooden cocktail sticks.

Place the stuffed duck in a plate or bowl, and steam for 80–90 minutes. Add some water about half-way through cooking. When cooked, remove the duck onto a flat ovenproof dish (everything up to this point can be done hours ahead). When ready to serve, put the duck in a preheated oven at 200°C/400°F/Gas Mark 6 for 30 minutes and then put it under the grill for 5 minutes to get a good brown colour. Put the cooking juices in a small saucepan and leave undisturbed for a few minutes so that the oil separates from the juice. Discard the oil and heat the juice to be used as a pouring sauce.

Carve the duck western-style if you wish, and divide the stuffing equally. This dish can be eaten hot, warm or cold.

Fish Cooked in Tamarind

This fish is to be eaten cold the day after cooking. Substitute lemon juice for tamarind (page 20) if you wish. The fish will still taste beautifully hot and sour and will be very good as a lunch dish with a green salad and brown bread. In the island of Sulawesi in Indonesia, where this dish originated, sliced red tomatoes are used generously to garnish the fish. Use whole mackerel or fresh tuna steaks.

Serves 6–8

mackerel or fresh tuna steaks weighing about 2 kg (4 lb)
1 teaspoon ground turmeric
1 teaspoon salt
10 large red chillies, seeded and sliced thin diagonally
15 shallots or 4 onions, finely sliced
6 cloves garlic, finely sliced
5-cm (2-inch) piece of ginger, thinly sliced
300 ml (½ pint) tamarind water or lemon juice
more salt to taste
tomato slices to garnish

Clean the fish and rub them with the turmeric and salt. Mix all the sliced ingredients together, and lay half of them at the bottom of a saucepan that will accommodate the fish in a single layer. Put the fish on top of these, then spread the remaining sliced ingredients on top of the fish. Add some salt to the tamarind water or lemon juice, to taste, and pour this over the fish. Cover the pan and cook slowly for 25–30 minutes. Shake the pan gently from time to time and make sure that the fish is not burnt. You can add a little more water during cooking if you think the fish is becoming too dry and is in danger of burning. When the cooking is complete, leave the fish to cool in the covered pan. When cold store in the refrigerator until next day.

Discard all the sliced ingredients just before serving the fish, garnished with tomato slices.

Fish Stuffed with Vegetables

When you ask your fishmonger to clean the fish, ask him to cut the backs and not the bellies as they are going to be stuffed from the back after the backbone and all the small bones are removed.

If you are cleaning and boning the fish yourself, proceed as follows: descale the fish first, then with a sharp knife cut along each side of the backbone, ease it out, and with scissors cut the backbone at the head and tail ends. Remove the guts and then the gills by pulling them out hard with your fingers. The next step is to remove the small bones carefully. Wash the fish inside and outside under the cold tap.

Serves 8

8 small trout, weighing about 140 g (6 oz) each or less
2 large onions, finely sliced, to line the baking tray
2 tablespoons chopped chervil or parsley

For the stuffing
2 tablespoons groundnut or olive oil
1 large onion, finely chopped
250 g (8 oz) carrots, peeled and diced
500 g (1 lb) button mushrooms, thinly sliced
½ teaspoon coarsely-ground black pepper
¼ teaspoon freshly-grated nutmeg
120 ml (4 fl oz) water
1 tablespoon tomato purée
1 tablespoon lime juice
1 teaspoon salt

Heat the oven to 180°C/350°F/Gas Mark 4.

To prepare the stuffing, start by heating the oil in a wok or saucepan. When it is hot, fry the chopped onion, stirring all the time, until soft. Add the carrots and mushrooms, stir for 2 minutes, then add the rest of the ingredients except the chervil or parsley. Stir again, cover the pan and simmer for 3–4 minutes, taking care not to let the stuffing dry out completely and burn. Adjust the seasoning and leave to cool.

Butter a baking tray and spread the sliced onions evenly on it. Place the fish, upright on their bellies, next to each other, but not touching, on top of the onions. Divide the stuffing equally among the fish. Scatter the chervil or parsley on top, cover the fish with buttered aluminium foil, and bake in the oven for 40–45 minutes. Serve hot or cold.

Skate Wings with Chinese Chives and Coconut Cream

Chinese chives are available pretty well all year round in oriental shops. They are stronger-tasting than ordinary chives. When you cannot get them and ordinary garden chives are not in season, replace them with the green parts of spring onions.

Try to get skate wings that are not too large, so that you won't need to cut them and one piece will be the right size for one portion. You can substitute double or single cream for the coconut cream.

Serves 4

4 skate wings

For the sauce
2 tablespoons groundnut or olive oil
2 shallots, finely chopped
1 clove garlic, finely chopped
2 green chillies, seeded and very finely diced
1 carrot, peeled and very finely diced
1 teaspoon very finely-diced ginger
8 tablespoons hot water
300 ml (½ pint) coconut cream or double or single cream
salt and pepper to taste
1 tablespoon lime or lemon juice
2–3 tablespoons chopped Chinese chives

Heat the oil in a frying pan and fry all the chopped and diced ingredients for the sauce for 3 minutes, stirring continuously. Then add the water, bring it to the boil and when boiling add the skate wings. Stir and continue cooking with the pan covered for 3 minutes. Uncover the pan, turn the skate wings over and add the cream, and salt and pepper to taste.

Cook for 1 minute more, stirring so that the skate wings are well coated with the sauce. Mix in the lime or lemon juice and chives. Adjust the seasoning and stir for just one more minute. Serve immediately with new potatoes or pasta, and freshly-steamed vegetables.

Stuffed Squid

Stuffing squids is so much easier than stuffing vegetables, because the body of the squid seems to have been planned for the purpose. The Indonesians, Vietnamese, Filipinos and others have different combinations of ingredients for the stuffing. Here is one that I use so often I have forgotten its origin.

Serves 4–6

4 squid, about 250–275 g (8–9 oz) each

For the stuffing
2 shallots, finely chopped
2 cloves garlic, finely chopped
1 teaspoon finely-chopped ginger
2 tablespoons groundnut or olive oil
½ teaspoon chilli powder or ground black pepper
125 g (4 oz) tenderloin of pork, minced
125 g (4 oz) raw prawns, without shells, deveined then minced
3 tablespoons desiccated coconut or breadcrumbs
6–8 tablespoons hot water
1 egg, beaten (optional)
½ teaspoon salt
2 tablespoons chopped coriander leaves or parsley

For the sauce
3 tablespoons groundnut or olive oil
1 small onion, finely chopped
2 cloves garlic, finely chopped
1 teaspoon ground coriander
5–6 ripe tomatoes, peeled and chopped
1 tablespoon fish sauce or light soy sauce
3 tablespoons *mirin* (Japanese rice wine) or white wine
125 ml (4 fl oz) water
salt and pepper to taste

Clean the squid, discarding the ink sacs and the heads. Chop the tentacles finely, to use in the stuffing.

Cook the stuffing. Fry the shallots, garlic and ginger in the oil, stirring all the time, for 2 minutes. Add the chilli powder or black pepper, the minced pork, prawns and the tentacles. Stir-fry for 1–2 minutes. Then add the rest of the ingredients for the stuffing, except the egg and the coriander leaves or parsley. Continue cooking until all the liquid has been absorbed, and the stuffing is moist. Adjust the seasoning and leave to cool before adding the egg (if used) and the coriander leaves or parsley and stuffing the mixture into the squid.

Do not stuff the squid too full as the stuffing will expand a little. Close the openings with cocktail sticks.

The squid are cooked in the sauce in a large saucepan, big enough to put them side by side. Heat the oil and brown the squid on both sides in the oil. Transfer them to a plate and keep aside while you continue with the sauce. Add the chopped onion and garlic to the pan, fry for 1 minute and add the rest of the ingredients. Simmer for another minute and put the squid back into the pan. Cover the pan and simmer for 16–18 minutes, adding more liquid if necessary. Uncover the pan, turn up the flame and cook the squid in the boiling sauce for 2 more minutes. Cut the squid diagonally into thick slices on a serving dish, pour the sauce over them and serve straight away.

Monkfish in Curry Sauce with Yogurt

I use monkfish for several of the recipes in this book because the flesh is firm and will absorb any sauce well. Also, it is free of small bones.

Serves 4

2 monkfish tails weighing about 1 kg (2 lb) in all (with bones)
1 tablespoon lime juice
¼ teaspoon salt

For the paste
2 tablespoons groundnut oil
2 shallots, chopped
2 cloves garlic, chopped
2 large green chillies, seeded and chopped
1 teaspoon chopped ginger
1 green cardamom
1 teaspoon ground coriander
½ teaspoon ground cumin
½ teaspoon ground turmeric
¼ teaspoon ground cinnamon
¼ teaspoon grated nutmeg
4 tablespoons water

To be added later
150 ml (¼ pint) fish stock
salt and pepper to taste
175 ml (6 fl oz) unsweetened yogurt
2 tablespoons chopped coriander leaves or mint

Fillet the monkfish and use the bones to make stock. Cut each fillet into 4 pieces. Rub these with the lime juice and salt and keep aside.

Put all the ingredients for the paste in a blender and blend until smooth. Transfer this into a saucepan and boil, stirring all the time, for 4 minutes. Add the fish stock and salt and pepper. Continue cooking the curry sauce for 2–3 more minutes, then add the yogurt, a spoonful at a time, stirring all the while. Adjust the seasoning. Add the fish pieces, stir again gently and simmer for 2–3 minutes. Add the chopped coriander or mint, cover the pan for 30 seconds. Remove from heat and serve immediately with rice or pasta.

Steamed Tuna Steaks with Hot and Sour Vegetables

Here the fish is steamed over a bed of lettuce leaves and plenty of sliced onions, then covered with the hot and sour vegetables.

Serves 4

1 kg (2 lb) tuna fish cut into 4 steaks
2 tablespoons lime or lemon juice
¼ teaspoon salt
¼ teaspoon chilli powder
4 onions, finely sliced
2–3 tablespoons groundnut oil
2 round or cos lettuces, washed and roughly shredded

For the hot and sour vegetables
2 shallots, finely chopped
2 garlic cloves, finely chopped
4 large red chillies, seeded and chopped
1 teaspoon finely-chopped ginger
2 tablespoons vegetable or groundnut oil
1 teaspoon ground coriander
4 carrots, diced
1 turnip (about 100 g/3½ oz), diced
2 small green mangoes or apples, cored and diced, and kept in slightly
    salted water
½ teaspoon ground white pepper
2 tablespoons rice or white wine vinegar

Rub the tuna fish with lime or lemon juice, salt and chilli powder. Keep in a cool place. Fry the onions in the oil until soft. Transfer to a large saucepan and put the lettuce leaves on top of the onion; then arrange the fish on top of the lettuce. Cover the saucepan and place it on a medium heat for 8 minutes while you cook the vegetables in another saucepan or wok.

Fry the shallots, garlic, chillies and ginger in the oil for 2 minutes, stirring all the time. Add the ground coriander, carrots, turnip, and mangoes or apples. Stir-fry for one minute, then add the pepper and vinegar. Keep stirring for another 2 minutes, then transfer these to the other saucepan, laying them on top of the fish. Cover the pan again and continue cooking slowly for 15–20 minutes. Turn off the heat but keep the cover on the pan for 4 or 5 minutes. Serve the fish with the vegetables divided equally among them. You can also include some of the onions.

Condiments and Relishes

Here are some traditional sauces, relishes and condiments to complement the South-East Asian flavours of the dishes given in this book. Most of them have equivalents that you can buy in jars, bottles or plastic tubs from oriental shops and supermarkets, and these are often of excellent quality; but, as always, the one you make at home often tastes the best.

Peanut Sauce

This peanut sauce is better known in South-East Asia as a satay sauce. Each country has its own favourite combination of spices used in it. You can buy it ready-made now from supermarkets and ethnic shops, but most of them contain too much thickening and MSG and taste bland. Some oriental shops also sell a ready-prepared powdered satay sauce mix.

It is not difficult to make, and here is the basic recipe for it. Increase the amount of chilli if you wish, but be very cautious about increasing the amounts of the spices.

120 ml (4 fl oz) vegetable oil
250 g (8 oz) raw peanuts

For the paste
3 shallots, chopped
3 cloves garlic, chopped
1-cm (½-inch) piece of shrimp paste (optional)
1 teaspoon chopped ginger
2 large red chillies, seeded and chopped, or ½ teaspoon chilli powder

1 teaspoon ground coriander
½ teaspoon ground cumin
2 tablespoons dark soy sauce
2 tablespoons tamarind water or lemon juice
3 tablespoons groundnut oil

500 ml (18 fl oz) water
salt and pepper

Heat the oil in a wok or frying pan and fry the peanuts, stirring all the time, for 4 minutes. Remove with a slotted spoon to drain in a colander. Leave to cool. When cool, grind the peanuts into a fine powder in a blender or coffee grinder. Discard the oil.

Put all the ingredients for the paste in a blender and blend until smooth. Transfer into a saucepan and cook, stirring all the time, for 4 minutes. Add the water and season with salt and pepper. Bring it to the boil, give it a stir when boiling, and add the ground peanuts. Simmer, stirring often, for 8–10 minutes until the sauce becomes thick. Adjust the seasoning and serve straight away.

If you are keeping the sauce for later use, let it cool and store it in a jar in the fridge. It will stay good in the fridge for about a week.

This peanut sauce can be frozen for up to 2 months. Thaw out completely before reheating it for immediate use.

Prawn Balachaung

This is a Burmese relish that can be eaten with raw or steamed vegetables as an accompaniment to rice. Here it is also used as one of the ingredients of the Burmese chicken curry on page 177. *Balachaung* is available in small jars in most oriental shops. It is usually very hot and garlicky.

The prawns used here are the small dried prawns, also called dried shrimps, sold in packets in oriental shops.

250 g (8 oz) dried prawns (dried shrimps)
3 tablespoons vegetable oil
2 onions, very finely chopped
8 cloves garlic, very finely sliced
1 tablespoon sesame oil
3 red or green chillies, seeded and very finely chopped, or 1 teaspoon chilli powder

2 teaspoons finely-chopped ginger
½ teaspoon ground turmeric
1 teaspoon shrimp paste (optional)
juice of 2 limes or lemons
¼ teaspoon salt

Soak the dried prawns in warm water for 10 minutes. Drain, and chop them very finely. This process can also be done in a food processor or blender. Keep aside.

Heat the vegetable oil in a wok or frying pan, and fry the chopped onions and garlic until they are just becoming slightly brown. Take these out with a slotted spoon and reserve. Add the sesame oil to the wok or pan and fry the rest of the ingredients except the lime or lemon juice, stirring all the time, for 2 minutes. Put in the ground prawns and continue stir-frying for 2 minutes. If the mixture looks as though it is getting too dry and is in danger of burning, add 2–3 tablespoonsful of water. Adjust the seasoning and add the fried onions and garlic. Continue stir-frying for a few more seconds or until the mixture is dry. Then add the lime or lemon juice. Give it another stir and take it off the heat. Leave to cool before storing it in a jar, then put it into the fridge.

Hot and Sour Chilli Relish

This relish is the standard hot chilli sauce served with soups in most South-East Asian countries. Most Asian restaurants add this chilli sauce to the soup bowls just before serving them to the customers. This is what makes the soups look oily on the top. If the sauce is served separately in a little bowl, the diners can take as much or as little as they wish.

3 tablespoons groundnut or vegetable oil
20–25 dried small chillies, soaked in water until soft, then drained
4 shallots, chopped
4 cloves garlic, chopped
juice from 3–4 limes or lemons
1 teaspoon sugar
2 tablespoons fish sauce
some salt if necessary

Heat the oil in a wok or frying pan, and fry the chillies, shallots and garlic, stirring all the time, for 4–5 minutes. Cool, then transfer them, including the oil, into a blender. Add the rest of the ingredients and blend until smooth. Taste, and add some salt if necessary. Transfer the relish into a bowl or a jar. Keep in the fridge until required, it will keep for up to 2 weeks.

Basic Fried Rice Mix

If you make fried rice often, this mixture is very convenient to have as you can make your fried rice much more quickly. In the food halls of some large department stores you can buy just the chilli mixture in jars, labelled *sambal nasi goreng*; usually it is a Dutch brand, often far too sweet. With it, you can get vacuum-packed dehydrated diced vegetables that you need to reconstitute before use.

Makes enough for 4 lots of fried rice, each sufficient for 4 people

4 tablespoons vegetable oil
2 onions, finely chopped
2 cloves garlic, finely chopped
4 large red chillies, seeded and finely chopped, or ½ teaspoon chilli
    powder
1 teaspoon finely-chopped ginger
500 g (1 lb) carrots, peeled and diced small
500 g (1 lb) button mushrooms, quartered or sliced
125 g (4 oz) shredded white cabbage
125 ml (4 fl oz) water
1 tablespoon paprika
2 tablespoons tomato purée
2 tablespoons light soy sauce
salt and pepper to taste

Heat the oil in a wok or a large shallow saucepan, and stir-fry the onions, garlic, chillies and ginger for 2 minutes. Then add the carrots, mushrooms and cabbage. Continue stir-frying for another minute, then add the water. Cover the wok or pan and simmer the mixture for 3 minutes. Uncover and add the rest of the ingredients. Continue cooking until the vegetables are cooked, about 3 more minutes. Cool and divide into four containers and keep in the fridge until required.

To make the fried rice, you just heat the mixture in a wok or large frying pan, add 1 tablespoon oil or butter and the cooked rice, and stir-fry until the rice is hot. (Fried rice recipe is on page 117.)

Chilli Bean Sauce

A very good and hot chilli bean sauce is available in Chinese shops. It is made with black and yellow bean sauce and is usually very hot and oily. I have not used chilli bean sauce for any of the recipes in this book, but it is a very convenient way of preserving the left-overs of the yellow bean sauce used for Halibut in garlic, ginger and yellow bean sauce (page 69). It is also a useful condiment to have with any noodle dishes that need to be spicier, and it is good for dipping any sort of crudités. It will keep for weeks in an airtight jar in the fridge.

2 tablespoons vegetable oil
1 teaspoon sesame oil
6 cloves garlic, finely chopped
2 teaspoons finely-chopped ginger
5 red or green chillies, finely chopped
125 ml (4 fl oz) water
1 tablespoon dark soy sauce
2 teaspoons sugar
175–200 g (6–7 oz) yellow bean sauce
2 teaspoons vinegar (optional)

Heat both kinds of oil in a wok or frying pan, stir-fry the garlic, ginger and chillies for 2 minutes, and add the water. Simmer for 3 minutes, then add the rest of the ingredients. Stir-fry these for a few seconds and continue to simmer for 2 more minutes. Stir it all around once more before taking it off the heat. Cool and store in an airtight jar in the fridge.

Vinegar Soy Sauce with Peanuts or Pine Nuts

For those who don't like any of the other sauces with chillies, this is good as a dipping sauce for miniature spring rolls and other canapés made with prawn paste.

    4 tablespoons mild vinegar
    3 tablespoons light soy sauce
    1 teaspoon finely-chopped ginger
    1 clove garlic, finely chopped (optional)
    2 tablespoons roasted peanuts or roasted pine nuts, roughly ground
    1 teaspoon sugar
    freshly-ground black pepper

Mix all these ingredients together in a small bowl, and serve.

Sweet Chilli Sauce

This type of chilli sauce is widely available in Thai shops under two different labels, one for chicken and the other for seafood. They are both quite hot and sweet, without any significant difference in taste. This is a good dipping sauce for spring rolls, steamed golden parcels and other canapés in this book. It is very easy to make yourself.

    175 ml (6 fl oz) water
    10–12 large red chillies, chopped
    3 cloves garlic
    2 teaspoons sugar
    ½ teaspoon salt
    1 tablespoon fish sauce
    1 tablespoon vinegar
    1 tablespoon groundnut or sunflower oil
    1 teaspoon sesame oil (optional)

Put all the ingredients in a saucepan and bring them to the boil. Cover the saucepan and simmer for 12–15 minutes. Transfer everything to a blender or food processor, and blend until smooth. Adjust the seasoning and transfer the sauce to a bowl or jar. Serve straight away or keep in the fridge for later use.

Chilli Fish Sauce

The countries of South-East Asia are pretty evenly divided between those that prefer fish sauce in their relishes and condiments and those that prefer soy sauce. For westerners who are not used to the pungent smell of fish sauce, soy sauce may be more attractive. Both sauces are often mixed with finely-chopped fresh bird chillies – the very small chillies that are considered to be the hottest of them all. They are now widely available in oriental shops.

Its main use is as a dipping sauce.

2 tablespoons fish sauce
2–3 bird chillies, finely chopped
a squeeze of lime or lemon juice

Mix these in a small bowl and serve.

Fried Onion Flakes

Most South-East Asian soups call for a sprinkling of onion flakes. These are quite time-consuming to make. Fortunately, they are available in oriental shops (imported from Thailand and Malaysia), and in supermarkets, imported from Copenhagen. Both types are packed in airtight plastic tubs.

But if you do want to make fried onion flakes yourself, I suggest you do it with shallots. They get crisp quicker, and they don't need to be floured as onions do.

500 g (1 lb) shallots, finely sliced
125 ml (4 fl oz) vegetable oil

Heat the oil in a wok and stir-fry the shallots in two batches until golden brown. Take them out with a large slotted spoon to drain on absorbent paper. They will become quite crisp when cold. Store in an airtight container until required.

Apple and Cucumber Acar with Beansprouts

Acar (pronounced 'atjar') is a generic term in many Asian countries for a dish of vegetables, plain or mixed, raw or cooked, lightly pickled with vinegar, and mildly or very highly spiced. A mildly-spiced *acar*, like this one, is a very good accompaniment for fish dishes and rich heavy meat dishes. This one can also be served as a side salad. The apples here are an alternative to green mangoes. Use mangoes if you prefer them and can get them.

For the dressing
100 ml (3½ fl oz) white distilled vinegar
2 shallots, finely sliced
1 green chilli, seeded and finely sliced, or 2–3 drops of Tabasco
1 teaspoon salt or a little more
2 tablespoons caster sugar
6 tablespoons warm water

1 large Bramley Seedling or 2 Cox's apples
1 cucumber
125 g (4 oz) beansprouts

First, mix all the ingredients for the dressing in a large glass bowl, so that you can put the sliced apples straight away into it to prevent discoloration. Adjust seasoning.

Peel the apples, core and quarter them, then slice them thinly. Put the slices into the dressing immediately. Peel the cucumber, cut it lengthways into two halves and scoop out the seeds. Slice the cucumber thinly and mix the slices with the dressing in the bowl. For this salad, the beansprouts' little brown roots need to be picked off and discarded, otherwise the *acar* will look messy. Mix all the ingredients together well in the bowl and keep in a cool place for at least 1 hour before serving.

You can also keep this *acar* in a large glass jar or bowl, tightly covered, in the fridge for several days.

Thai Cucumber Sauce

This is a variation of the apple and cucumber *acar* above. As it is Thai in
origin, it uses fish sauce and a lot of hot chillies. You can of course
reduce the quantity of chilli to suit your taste.

1 cucumber, peeled, halved lengthways and the seeds discarded, then
    sliced thin
3–4 bird chillies, finely chopped
2 tablespoons fish sauce
2 tablespoons white distilled vinegar
1 tablespoon sugar
1 tablespoon chopped chives or spring onions

Mix all the ingredients together in a glass bowl. Serve straight away or
reserve for later use. This will keep fresh in the fridge for up to 48 hours.

Kimchee

Another kind of *acar* or pickled vegetable. This is a variation of the
widely-known Korean pickled cabbage, and is a good accompaniment
to *Bulgogi* (Korean beef) on pages 94, 98. It takes several days to 'cure',
so start making it well in advance.

1 kg (2 lb) Chinese cabbage
1 tablespoon salt
50 g (2 oz) cayenne pepper
2 cloves garlic, crushed
1 bunch of spring onions, green part only, chopped
2 teaspoons sugar
1 teaspoon dried shrimps, soaked in warm water for 10 minutes, drained
    then chopped (optional)

Cut the cabbage crossways into 2.5-cm (1-inch) chunks. Mix well with
the salt in a colander and leave to drain for at least 30 minutes. Rinse
well and drain again. Then, in a large bowl, mix the cabbage with the
rest of the ingredients, and leave to 'cure' for 3–4 days in a cool and dark
place. Store in glass jars in the fridge until required.

Bibliography

Bissell, Frances, *Sainsbury's Book of Food*, Websters International Publishers for J. Sainsbury plc, London, 1988

Brennan, Jennifer, *Thai Cooking*, Jill Norman and Hobhouse, London, 1981

Cost, Bruce, *Foods from the Far East*, Century, London, 1988

Davidson, Alan, *Fish and Fish Dishes of Laos*, Charles E. Tuttle, Rutland and Tokyo, 1975

Davidson, Alan, *Seafood of South-East Asia*, Federal Publications, Singapore, 1977, and Macmillan, London, 1978

Davidson, Alan, *North Atlantic Seafood*, Macmillan, London, 1979

Grigson, Jane, *Fish Cookery*, International Wine and Food Publishing Company, 1973, and Penguin Books, 1975

Hill, Shaun, *Gidleigh Park Cookery Book*, Century, London, 1990

Holt, Geraldene, *The Gourmet Garden*, Pavilion Books, London, 1990

Khaing, Mi Mi, *Cook and Entertain the Burmese Way*, Karoma, Ann Arbor, 1978

Kritakara, M. L. Taw, and M. R. Pimsai Amranand, *Modern Thai Cooking*, Editions Duang Kamol, Bangkok, 1977

Owen, Sri, *The Home Book of Indonesian Cookery*, Faber, London, 1976

Owen, Sri, *Indonesian Food and Cookery*, Prospect Books, London, 2nd edition 1986

Owen, Sri, *Indonesian and Thai Cookery*, Piatkus, London, 1988

Owen, Sri, *The Cooking of Thailand, Indonesia and Malaysia*, Martin Books for J. Sainsbury plc, Cambridge, 1991

Phia Sing, edited by Alan and Jennifer Davidson, *Traditional Recipes of Laos*, Prospect Books, London, 1981

Round, Jeremy, *The Independent Cook*, Barrie and Jenkins, London, 1988

Routhier, Nicole, *The Foods of Vietnam*, Stewart, Tabori and Chang, New York, 1989

Shurtleff, William and Aoyagi, Akiko, *The Book of Tempeh*, Harper & Row, New York and Toronto, 1979

So, Yan-kit, *Yan-kit's Classic Chinese Cookbook*, Dorling Kindersley, London, 1984

So, Yan-kit, *Wok Cookbook*, Piatkus, London, 1985

Willan, Anne, *Real Food*, Macmillan, London, 1988

Willan, Anne, *Reader's Digest Complete Guide to Cookery*, Dorling Kindersley, London, 1989

Index